Dhoop Aane Do

Dhoop Aane Do

Pages Plucked from Memories

Gulzar

Translated from the Marathi by Ambarish Mishra

AMARYLLIS

AMARYLLIS

An imprint of Manjul Publishing House Pvt. Ltd.
• C-16, Sector 3, Noida, Uttar Pradesh 201 301, India
Website: www.manjulindia.com
Registered Office:
• 2nd Floor, Usha Preet Complex, 42 Malviya Nagar, Bhopal 462 003 – India
Distribution Centres
Ahmedabad, Bengaluru, Bhopal, Chennai, Hyderabad,
Kolkata, Mumbai, Noida, Pune

Dhoop Aane Do–Pages Plucked from Memories by Gulzar

First published in Marathi in 2022 by Arun Shevate,
Ruturang Prakashan, Mumbai. Published with permission from Gulzar.

Translated from the Marathi by Ambarish Mishra

This English edition first published in India in 2024

ISBN 978-93-5543-957-4

Cover Design: Neelima P Aryan

Inside illustrations by:
Gulzar: 156, 161, 162, 194
Satish Bhavsar: 28, 33, 39, 45, 52, 80-81, 160
Ramesh Thorat: 179

Printed and bound in India by Parksons Graphics Pvt. Ltd.

Farhana

My right hand with six fingers,

Farhana Mahmood!

Contents

A Word More...

India is a land of wonderful languages.

There are some major languages of some major regions; and numerous dialects merging into them—or emerging from them... Like rivers and rivulets spread all over the landscape of our country.

The articles in this collection appeared first in Marathi, thanks to Arun Shevate, in *Ruturang*, his literary annual magazine. Some translated from Urdu, Hindi and English, and some based on my interviews in *Hindustani*.

The subjects have been flowing from one language into another like river waters. Hence, they change their colours and shores of expression as per the language and the dialect.

Here it is in English in the hands of an accomplished boatman like Ambarish Mishra. He sails through English, Hindi and Marathi with remarkable ease. When he translates a piece, he does it in his own expression, and each word lands at the right place with every shade of meaning intact.

Farhana, with her six fingers, worked tirelessly on every version. She toiled 25x7, I mean it! on the book.

Thanks to Vikas for his enthusiasm, and Bidisha for dressing up the book so gracefully. Thanks to Avinash who managed our working hours with a watch!

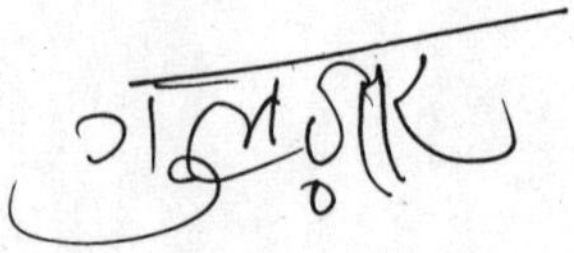

Translator's Note

This was sometime in June 2023.

My friend Arun Shevate, the editor of *Ruturang*, a Marathi literary annual, rang me up one sunny afternoon to say that Gulzar-ji wanted me to translate *Dhoop Aane Do* into English. Wow! It was indeed an honour to team up with one of India's much-respected, much-toasted literary figures.

As the first flush of euphoria receded, the enormity of the situation dawned on me: I was going to work with a difficult-to-please giant. A wizard of words. Post-Independence, India's best cultural chronicler.

My heart sank.

However, sessions with Gulzar-ji, over Kahwah or lemon tea, were educative and exhilarating as well. The master at work never ceased to amaze me. He would go through each article with a fine-toothed comb, weighing every word, calibrating every phrase, dotting the i's and crossing the t's with the ardour of a newsroom warhorse.

Each time Gulzar-ji suggested a change in the copy he would profusely apologise: '*Muaaf karo*, Ambarish, *thodi gustaakhi karoonga*.' Taskmaster he is, but an affectionate guru too.

Dhoop Aane Do is a unique book in that it is the culmination of an alliance between Urdu and Marathi. Every year the poet would speak at length, in Urdu, to *Ruturang*, on a topic of his choice. The spoken word was dressed up in Marathi by the *Ruturang* team for its annual issue.

My job was to see that not much is lost in translation given that the English version is twice removed from Gulzar-ji's exquisite Urdu. For four long months I was serenading three languages—all at one go, happily plundering their treasure troves for words, words and words. Gulzar-ji once described the exercise as *guftagu*—a difficult-to-translate term!

The book is a mélange of genres: short essays, memoirs, thumbnail sketches of friends and colleagues, anecdotes, travel notes, periodic musings, a free-wheeling interview and, above all, Gulzar-ji's enchanting poems.

Also, Gulzar-ji has experimented with biographical stories: a relatively new genre which blends facts with fiction to dramatise an incident drawn from the flux of life. 'Sahir and Jadu' and 'Kuldip Nayar and the Pir' best illustrate the point.

Dhoop Aane Do offers deep insights into Gulzar-ji's life and times. The autobiographical tone of the book is evident. Given Gulzar-ji's reluctance to write his life story, *Dhoop Aane Do* will, I hope, compensate readers for the loss.

A tapestry of tales woven with threads of ecstasy and agony, *Dhoop Aane Do* blends the past and the present with dexterity and lyrical sensitivity. Tomorrow is just a click away.

Hope readers will welcome the book.

My most respectful adaab to Gulzar-ji, who made the English version possible.

Warm regards to Arun-ji (Shevate), Vikas-ji (Rakheja) of Manjul Publishing House, Farhana, Gulzar-ji's indefatigable editorial assistant and Akash, my tech-savvy friend who helped me streamline the printouts.

Many thanks to Boskyana.

Ambarish Mishra,
Mumbai, October 2023

FOREWORD

Dhoop Aane Do is unique in that it is a compilation of articles and essays, based on Gulzar-ji's conversations with *Ruturang*, a Marathi literary annual which I launched from my residence, tucked away in one of the verdant bylanes of a Mumbai suburb, way back in 1992.

I had read most of Gulzar-ji's works. I called on him on a rain-soaked August afternoon in 1993. We met at his Bandra office.

Not only did he agree to write for *Ruturang*, but he also put me through the paces, asking a couple of questions which stemmed from his concern for Marathi literature. *Dhoop Aane Do* is the culmination of a guru-shishya alliance that has enriched me over the last three decades. It helped me understand the creative process of a genius.

As Gulzar-ji lacks fluency in Marathi he suggested a procedure. He would speak at length on a topic of his choice a month or two before the deadline. The meetings were held at Boskyana, his Pali Hill residence, over breakfast. I would be at Gulzar-ji's doorstep at 8 a.m. sharp—armed with my writing pad and a tape recorder.

Often, the wretched contraption would let me down. Gulzar-ji would be unruffled. Within a week or so he would go through the transcript very carefully and suggest changes, if any.

For me, the sessions with Gulzar-ji were akin to a carnival of literature. I would call it the 'Boskyana' lit-fest. He would contemplate on life and times—a kind of prolonged monologue, peppered with gentle humour and lovely anecdotes, and delivered in a rambling style, even as his grip on the subject remained firm. He seemed to me like a sufi mystic on a flying visit to the idyllic Pali Hill.

My heartfelt thanks to Gulzar-ji, the presiding deity of *Ruturang*, Mr Ambarish Mishra, who readily agreed to translate the book into English, and Farhana-ji, Gulzar-ji's remarkably efficient secretary. Many thanks to Manjul Publishing House.

Arun Shevate

Pancham

Pancham's memories have the mysterious fragrance of an autumn evening. The sweet smell still burns brightly.

I first met Pancham during the making of *Bandini*, Bimal Roy's 1963 film, which marked my debut in filmdom. The song '*Mora gora ang layeeley*', which I wrote for *Bandini*, was well received.

Actually, I had no great wish to be a film lyricist. I was working in a garage, and was doing well reading and writing, and meeting friends from the Indian People's Theatre Association. However, Bimal-da asked me to join him as assistant director. 'Leave the job immediately. Don't waste yourself in a garage,' he said.

Sachindev Burman (SD Burman) was a part of Bimal-da's unit. Pancham would be with his father carrying the 'dagga' (the larger drum of the tabla) like a dutiful pupil. We both hit it off like a house on fire; we were of the same age and shared our dreams, ambitions, secrets, our likes and dislikes.

Pancham was a glass of champagne. Full of life: young, brittle, hyperactive, excitable and restless. His passion for music transcended cultures and continents. This man is going to be a great music director, I said to myself. It didn't take me long to decide that Pancham would be my choice if I ever make a film.

I think we could create good songs because we worked at a leisurely pace. There were no 'sittings', a much-hyped word in the lexicon of Hindi cinema. Creating a song was not a mere assignment for us. We enjoyed doing a song.

We constantly provoked each other because we wished to do our best. We never repeated ourselves, never followed the well-trodden path and never believed in playing safe. Creativity was my festering wound and his too. Music healed us.

We walked together, ate and worked together; went on long drives, drank wine, smoked cigarettes, fought, laughed. All that would go to make a song.

As I look back, I realise that we were intertwined in a creative process which was both elevating and exhausting. People say our songs have a style and syntax of their own. This happened because we worked in perfect harmony and never encroached on each other's space. Pancham respected my creativity, and I, his.

The stars in the sky are friends, but each follows its own course, its fate. Ditto with me and Pancham. We were allies, but autonomous. Single, but hyphenated.

No false praise, no waah-waahs. There was lot of back-slapping, but no back-scratching. While working, we both were no-nonsense. That made a lot of sense.

Pancham would often drop in home. Unannounced. Often, I would go to his place. We never rushed each other. We would savour the process, note by note. The clock would stop ticking.

When on a long drive he would be humming a tune which he had set aside for me—his fingers tapping non-stop on the dashboard or the car's door.

Once my car stopped at a traffic intersection in suburban Mumbai. Pancham waved to me from his car. He seemed keen to talk. However, a car stood between his and mine. Look at Pancham's cheek. He asked the car owner to roll down his windows, which the poor fellow promptly did. While we both got talking, the man in the car kept looking at us both, from side to side. It was straight out of a Wimbledon match with eyeballs shifting from Federer to Nadal and vice versa.

Only Pancham could do this.

He once told me that he can 'see' a playback singer as he composes a song. 'I've often seen your *thobda* (face) too,' he added with a guffaw.

'But I am not a playback singer,' I protested.

'Arre baba, when I "see" your face, it means that you will write on this tune,' he explained in his pidgin Hindi. What more honour can there be?

Parichay (1972) was our first film. He was excited when I gave him the lyrics; he came to my place around midnight, and took me out on a long drive—and composed '*Musafir hoon yaaro, naa ghar hai, naa thikaana...*' as the car meandered along Mumbai's sleep-laced streets.

Salil Chowdhury did the music for *Mere Apne* (1971), my first film, while Madan Mohan did *Koshish* (1972). They were producer NC Sippy's choice much before I came on the scene. Thus I had no say in the matter. Also, a debutant director cannot dictate terms to the producer.

However, during *Parichay*, I didn't think twice before signing up Pancham. I knew he would do a great job, and I must say that Pancham lived up to our mutual expectation.

Next was *Aandhi* in 1975—a poignant, nuanced tale of an elderly, intelligent couple. The songs were neatly woven into the story. Although not proficient in Hindi, Pancham understood poetry. Also, he had a feel for words—their rhythm, meaning, metre and cadence.

Pancham asked no questions while doing '*Is moad se jaate hain...*' However, no sooner was he through with the song than he asked me with child-like naiveté, 'Gulzar, where the hell is this place called *nasheman*?'

I suspect he probably thought nasheman was a tourist spot. 'Pancham, nasheman is the Urdu word for nest,' I told him. Nevertheless, he could sense the word's beauty and cadence—and this reflects in the composition.

In 1975 we were recording '*O...maanjhi re...*' from *Khushboo*. For no rhyme or reason, Pancham stopped the recording midway and asked his assistant Manohari-da to get two soda bottles.

'What? Soda bottles? For what?'

Manohari-da tried to probe, but Pancham kept mum. Finally, the bottles arrived. Scotch will soon follow, I said to myself. Pancham emptied the bottles and got them filled with water at varying levels. He then blew air into them to create the sound of a steam engine. Basu Chakravarty was assigned the task. All his life Pancham was pre-occupied with sound, its moods and manifestations.

'*Do naino mein aansoo bhare hain*' from *Khushboo* is, I think, one of Pancham's finest numbers. I liked the tune immensely. The song was recorded in Lata-ji's voice. But too many instruments and Lata-ji's high pitch didn't go well with the song. It hardly sounded like a lullaby. I told Pancham to re-record it. He said nothing.

It so happened that Lata didi was to record a song for my next film *Ghar*. On the sidelines I spoke to her about '*Do naino mein aansoo bhare hain*'. She agreed to do it again. A vibraphone was used to enhance the beauty of the song. The second take was used in the film, while the first one has been included in the CD.

The *Ghar* song had a line '*Aap ki badmaashiyon ke yeh naye andaz hain*'. Pancham was a tad nervous. He said, 'Lata didi would take exception to badmaashiyon.'

'What's wrong with the word?' I asked.

Pancham replied, 'You see, Gulzar... badmaashiyon sounds indecent, no? Didi wouldn't like it.'

'Relax,' I said, 'If anything goes wrong, I'll change the word.'

Rehearsals done, we asked Lata didi about the song. 'It's a nice number, perfect,' she replied. I told her about badmaashiyon. Didi laughed and said, 'Well, I've been singing all kinds of songs over the years. I've never met this word before in a song.' Pancham didn't know where to look.

Kitaab (1977) has the long-distance train as one of its characters. A scene in the film shows the engine driver extolling his wife's virtues. I wrote a simple song: '*Dhanno ki aankhon mein...*'

Pancham set it to tune and sang it. I realised that he should sing it for the film as well. It was his song. He agreed. '*Dhanno ki aankhon mein*' has blended seamlessly with the scene.

Despite his hectic schedule Pancham found time to go to

the States. This was sometime in the mid-1970s. He returned with a funky instrument—flanger. It produced a novel sound—something like, for instance, '*tui...tui...tui*'. He was keen on using it for '*Dhanno ki aankhon mein...*'.

The idea was that the instrument would accompany the train as the background score each time the locomotive chugged across the screen. He further said that the flanger sound would be around since the start of the film so that it could blend with the pace of the train. I must say that I liked Pancham's idea—although I was apprehensive initially.

There was one more lullaby in *Kitaab*. I must have been thinking of my mother when I wrote '*Hari, din toh beeta*'. She would be singing, cooking or washing. Dina Pathak played the role in *Kitaab*. I wanted a voice which would sound like a simple, elderly Indian woman steeped in tradition.

Well-known singer Rajkumari's son Dube was part of our editing team. I asked him if his mother would sing '*Hari, din toh beeta...*'

Dube was happy. 'She will, Sir,' he said.

Pancham's tune suited Rajkumari-ji's voice, and, needless to add, she sang exceedingly well. We recorded one more song in Rajkumari-ji's voice—'*More sainyyaji utarenge paar ho*', which has been used in *Kinara* (1977) as background score.

'*Aa, Aaa, Eie, Eiee, Master-ji ki aayee chitthi...*' is a fun song from *Kitaab* (1977) by school children all set to rag the teacher. Pancham wanted a beat akin to the thumping of desks. All tables and desks in the studio were clubbed together and Pancham went bang, bang, bang... thump, thump, thump, testing each table. Finally, he chose a few for the take. The beat was segued into the song.

Writing children's songs is a tough task because elders can't think like toddlers. I love writing for children as there is still a 'child' in me. Penning a nonsense poem comes easy to me.

In *Kitaab*, there is this fat, dim-witted boy who makes a mess of whatever he does. He wants to join the song, '*Aa, Aaa, Eie, Eiee, Master-ji ki aayee chitthi*', but can't sing to save his life; he is out of tune. I borrowed a line from the VIP underwear ad which the boy lip-synced—and the song made a powerful impact.

'*Ek hi khwaab kayee bar dekha*', the *Kinara* song, has an interesting story. Words began to buzz in my mind as I was writing the script: '*Ek hi khwaab kayee baar dekha...*' I wrote the lines on a piece of paper and gave it to Pancham; he kept it aside, saying, 'We'll do this later.' Some more songs were recorded and I reminded him about '*Ek hi khwaab...*'

'We'll do it, yaar. Where is the hurry?'

And then he sat down to do the song—what a great composition! After the take, Pancham asked Bhupendra Singh to put on the headphones, handed the guitar to him and asked him to play. Bhupinder had not had a single rehearsal. Just play, Pancham told him.

While playing Bhupendra struck another note, slightly off-key, and Pancham wanted to record it again. I stopped him, saying that I was going to retain the strokes in the film. If you watch *Kinara*, you will find Hema Malini, who is playing cards with Dharmendra-ji, kissing the card in her hand exactly when Bhupendra's guitar goes off-key. Pancham saw the film and was happy.

I made *Musafir* (1986) with Dr Jabbar Patel. I wrote the screenplay, which was loosely based on Vijay Tendulkar's two plays. We were working on the song '*Main thak gaya hoon...*' Pancham wanted to know if there was a river somewhere near the outdoor location.

'Why?' I asked.

'Actually, I am wondering if I can weave a dhrupad-like line into the boatman's song,' he said.

'Go ahead, do it,' I said.

Pancham was not just a tunesmith; he knew the bare basics of film-making as well. He could go beyond his own craft and contemplate on the aesthetics and architecture of cinema. When he was in the recording studio, myriad ideas would float in the air, and simultaneously, I would begin to imagine how to shoot the song.

During the making of *Ijaazat* (1987), I called on Pancham at his residence. He played several Western notes for me. 'It's mind-blowing—look how it goes; as if one has taken a turn and come back to the same notes. See, it goes "*tee ree ree raa raa ree ree*",' he explained.

He asked me to write the words. I wrote: '*Chhoti si kahani se, baarishon ke paani se.*' Pancham hummed the lines again and again, and the song began to take shape. And before we could realise it, the entire song, with words and the tune, was ready.

Pancham insisted that the song should be included in *Ijaazat*. Not possible—there is no room for one more song, I said. He wouldn't give up. I too had liked the song. After much brainstorming we used it as the film's title song.

I asked my director of photography, Ashok Mehta, to capture with his camera raindrops at different spots. We went off to Khandala and came back with some breathtaking shots.

'*Mera kuchh samaan padha hai*' has an interesting story

behind it. When I gave the song to Pancham, he remarked wryly, 'Nice scene, I say.'

'Pancham, this is a song and not a film scene. You have to do the tune,' I retorted.

He was miffed. 'Tomorrow you will come to me with the *Times of India* and ask me to set it to tune,' he said, and set aside the song sheet. Asha-ji, who was sitting next to Pancham, picked it up, read it and began to hum the first line. Just like that.

Pancham caught her words '*Lauta do...*' He liked the way she was humming it. More such humming, and Pancham remarked, 'Looks good.' He then took the song sheet from Asha-ji, pulled the harmonium and, in a couple of minutes, '*Mera kuchh samaan tumhare paas padha hai*' came to life.

Being a blue-blooded Bengali, Pancham lacked fluency in Hindi, but he could unravel the sensitivity of a song. On reading '*Katra katra jeene do*,' also from *Ijaazat*, he said, 'Gulzar, have you ever heard a film song beginning with such words? You write according to your whim and then you want a tune from me. Please change the words—give me a nice, little word for the mukhda.'

'Don't get upset. If you insist. I'll change them,' I tried to pacify him. I suggested '*sawan bhaadon*' and '*boond boond*'. 'Good,' he exclaimed, 'see, these are musical words.' However, he soon realised that the new words didn't fuse with the song's mood and rhythm. He was struggling hard.

I didn't utter a word; I knew Pancham would be restless as long as the right tune eluded him. However, he would take off once he touched the core of the song, I told myself. After all, Pancham was Pancham.

After much huffing and puffing Pancham came back to my

original words—*Katra katra*. 'Easy on the ear, these words. Let me try,' he said as his fingers moved gracefully on the keyboard. He began to hum in many different ways and styles. And '*Katra katra*', lustrous and beautiful, was ready to be a part of Hindi cinema's folklore.

I was keen to attend the recording of '*Katra katra*'. Pancham was reluctant. I told him that my shooting schedule has been planned, and that I must decide how to shoot the song. I need to first 'see' the song in order to visualise it. Pancham brushed aside my suggestion. He said, '*Tum fikar mat karo*, Gulzar. You will get what you want.'

Strangely, Pancham was recording only half the line of '*Katra katra*'—also, he would skip one line and go to the next. What's going on, I asked myself. I tried to talk to him. He stopped me with a wave of his hand. 'Haven't I done justice to your songs which read like newspaper reports? I am doing something different; don't disturb me,' he said.

Next, Pancham recorded on another track the lines he had skipped, and later mixed the two tracks, luring viewers into believing that the song was being sung simultaneously by two female leads. I was amazed. It was a marvellous experiment of the 'double voice' technique.

Fixing his eyes on me, Pancham said, 'Look, I've done my job; now let me see what you do. You've always been challenging my creativity; now it's my turn.' We provoked each other to come up with our best.

It often happens that a film-maker can't include every song in the film. I had a clutch of such songs eager to see the light of day. I thought of doing a separate album of such 'homeless' songs.

Asha-ji backed the proposal; Pancham was reluctant, though. Me and Asha-ji kept persuading him, but he began to procrastinate. 'Let me finish this task and we will get going with your "*bekaar kaam*",' he would remark jokingly.

Thus happened *Dil Padosi Hai* (1987). We experimented with new ideas. Take, for instance, the song *'Raat Christmas Ki Thi'*. A man meets a woman, and both begin to see possibilities of an extra-marital relationship—an unconventional idea. Today, we see such couples around us; but back in the 1980s, no one would've thought of turning it into a film song, much less a private album. We did it.

Our films cannot do without stereotypes and cliches. Even senior couples are made to lip-sync calf-love ditties. There are no songs which mirror the mood of the changing times. *Dil Padosi Hai* was one such attempt.

Remember '*Jaane do, mujhe jaane do*' from the album? It talks of a woman trapped in an unhappy alliance. A victim of domestic violence, she wants to leave her husband. The break-up will certainly hurt the man, but she hopes that he will come out of it sooner or later. Hence, the line,

Thodi khalish hogi, thodasa gham hoga
Tanhaiee toh hogi, ehsaas kam hoga

The next moment she remembers incidents of domestic violence and says,

Gahari kharrashon ki gahari nishaaniyaan hain
Chehere ke neeche, kitni saari kahaniyaan hain

The song *'Maanjhi re maanjhi'*, also from the same album, is a kind of ode to a young girl who is ready to elope with her lover.

Knowing how tough the task is, she says that a jogi is going to meet her near the river—just a pretext.

It was a novel song. Pancham experimented with instruments to delineate its contours; the orchestration was mind-blowing. *Dil Padosi Hai* may have received a lukewarm response when it was released in 1987, but three decades later, connoisseurs are talking about it with fondness.

Pancham was open to new ideas, new interpretations. So was I. He followed his heart, his conscience. So did I. He would turn a musical phrase on its head. I did ditto with words and images. Destiny brought us together. Time sealed the pact.

Some of Pancham's peers were better than him. Yet, his songs were unique. He created a style, a genre of his own. While doing *'Khaali haath shaam aayee hai'*, Pancham made an off-the-cuff remark: 'Gulzar, this sounds like a Madan Mohan composition.' It was true. Set in the ghazal format, the song seems like Madan Mohan's composition. However, by the time *'Khaali haath shaam aayee hai'* was recorded, Pancham had engraved his name on it.

Pancham had his own eccentricities. For instance, if the tea was too hot, he would pour some cold water in the cup and gulp it down happily. He would place a clove on a burning cigarette and take a deep drag, saying, 'This doesn't affect the vocal chords!'

Pancham loved cooking and football. He had a formidable collection of video cassettes of landmark films. If a friend asked for a cassette, Pancham would write down his name in a ledger, and make life miserable for the borrower till he returned it. He was possessive about his cassette collection.

Every evening, he would go into a huddle with his musicians.

His close aide Bharat Ashar would supervise all arrangements. Every musician had a microphone placed before him and every note was recorded.

Ashar would be ready with earlier tapes should Pancham ask for one. Thus equipped, Pancham would create a tune with the help of 'dummy' words—sometimes he would use cuss-words too for fun—and send the audio tape to me. SaReGaMa has brought out a set of such records, titled *Gulzar–Pancham*.

Once he was slaving over a tune for one of my films. Finally, he sent me the tape—an exceptionally melodious song it was, I must say. It began with a one-line message recorded in Pancham's voice—'*Huzoor, isey zara nosh farmaaiyey.*' Pancham had got it all wrong. He had used the high-falutin' phrase just to show off. The tape ended with yet another Pancham message: 'Now the ball is in your court.'

Pancham was unbelievable. He is unforgettable.

Sagey Saare

Life's journey becomes much more pleasant because of friends with whom you break bread and share your ideas and idli! There are some I didn't have the privilege to meet, but have remained close to me—all kindred souls. Grace, for example. We remained in touch, shared many a poetic moment, without meeting. And when we met…

Grace

Renowned Marathi poet, much admired for his style and mesmerising imagery. Our first meeting took place when he was battling cancer, but we got on like a house on fire.

Even if I ask you not to go away, you wouldn't stop
You were getting ready for your final journey,
Doing the packing—which, anyway, you were going to leave here,
Bottles of poems have all been filled and sealed.

Grace, you've said all that you wanted to,
No more imploring, no seeking apologies;
You once said, 'Naked swords prick my back'
Who made you sleep on naked swords?

Pakde jaate hain farishton key likhe par
Aadmi koiee humara dum-e-tehreer bhi tha?—Ghalib

Grace, we both knew
That you were to go away that same night, or the following day,
The shadow of Time was lurking around

You recited some Urdu couplets

So did I,
Both worried that should we stop conversing
It would be time to say goodbye
Forever...

I unlocked my hand from yours,
What more would I say
And you too—while taking leave?
As you scrambled up the staircase of the past
Our hands entwined;
You said, as only you would:
'Next time get me your new poem';

I have come with a poem, Grace—
Would you listen?

Om Puri

Om Puri loved to feast on Rusk toasts with hot tea—whether at home or away from home.

Whenever he walked past my Pali Hill home, he would take a tea break. I had to keep ready for him a box of toasts. Looking for a good bakery was an additional task. Om had a whole list of them.

He soon found a bakery for himself. My search is on.

Have you seen a large bakery oven?
The door is shut tight and the dough, neatly arranged in trays, is allowed to bake;
Yesterday he too was brought in a trolley
Lumped, like dough, in the electric oven and the door was shut.

To be baked
What you get? A handful of ash

Sanjeev Kumar

There never was a more handsome young actor, who looked so nice as an old man, than him. He was all of twenty-three when he played the father's role in Henrik Ibsen's *All My Sons.* Renowned actor Leela Chitnis played his wife. I met Haribhai much before we both entered the world of glitz, glamour and greasepaint.

Back then, we used to keep lending and borrowing four annas or eight annas. Inflation was well under control. In later years we began to make good money. Hari's standing orders to me were loud and clear: 'Keep for me a bottle of Black Label. I may storm into your house any time at night after the shoot. And a non-veg dish too.' He belonged to a strictly 'veg-only' family.

We used to share our dark secrets and sunny hopes—bald truths which one doesn't put on the clothesline for drying.

During the shoot of *Parichay* once, he surprised me with an extraordinary act in a shot.

'Ask for a gift.'

I asked him.

'Give up "paan".'

Surprised, but I did. I have never had one, since then.

The year has evaporated as does the Haley's Comet
But it hasn't ended,
For long will one feel its icy, tornado-like onslaught;

Sanjeev has just left
His breath keeps swirling around me;
The dent in the cushion is still there
The date has changed, the page hasn't been turned as yet

Bapu

Bapu was 'Bapu'. I have seen him from close quarters. Heard his speeches, which he made every day at his prayer meetings in Delhi's Birla House. I would often sit with my Abbu by the radio, eager to listen to Bapu's broadcast.

Wrapped in just one-and-a-half-yard sky
And a loin cloth,
He had set out for his prayers
Someone blocked his path and placed a pistol on his chest,
Said, 'We don't agree with your thoughts.'
The pistol continues to spray bullets
Bapu's thoughts refuse to die

Rajiv Gandhi

I had once visited a factory at Andheri, a bustling Mumbai suburb, which manufactured electronic gadgets. I met a young pilot there. We had a nice chat. He gave me a few suggestions, which I readily accepted, on the music equipment I wanted to buy. We shook hands and he left.

Indubhai, the factory owner, told me that the pilot was none other than Rajiv Gandhi.

Later, I met Rajiv-ji when he was the country's prime minister. Young, handsome and graceful. His untimely death was both tragic and sad.

A sunbeam and its shadow
Everyone saw the sunbeam scaling dizzy heights—
The path was hard and slippery
Too many treacherous bends—and hollow trees

At the roots of which lurked Time's broken teeth
The shadow was tired—gasping for breath
Everyone tried to stop the sunbeam,
But he was a slice of radiance resplendent with gorgeous youth and freshness;
Everyone watched him with bated breath
And hoped he would reach the mountain top
And bring down on earth the twenty-first century;

A sudden, terrible explosion
A moment torn asunder—
The sunbeam was roasted alive
Dragged by fragments of fire, it fell into a deep valley

Namdeo Dhasal

Never before did I see such a huge turnout at a poet's funeral. Namdeo Dhasal was the poet of the people. Even the flames of the pyre couldn't extinguish the raw ardour of his poetry. He led the Dalit Panther Movement which altered the literary scene. When we met, we would make it a point to discuss the works of other poets and writers. Rarely did I recite my poems to him, or he to me. His death burned a deep hole in my consciousness.

I had to take a long detour
Actually, the cremation ground was not far away from my home,

It was a huge, black-and-white chessboard
Chock-a-block with rooks, knights and queens

And around them were pawns like me,
I was knocked off in the very first move

The one who placed me on the gameboard,
Had fettered my hands in the chain of faith
Knotted strings and amulets tied around my wrist
She had set the rules, and had planned my movement
So many footfalls on the chessboard
No space to place my foot,

How do I walk? Where do I go?

Threats dragged me further,
Fear accelerated my pace
I've met Gods everywhere
Bones would ache when they would place their hand
On my shoulder,
More worried about the other world than
The pressures of 'now' and 'here',
No more moves which will let me live
Maybe I chose a wrong path,
Actually, the cremation ground was not very far

VW Shirwadkar

The literary world knows him as Kusumagraj. A prolific writer, he has written poetry, fiction and plays. *Nata Samraat*, his landmark play which delineates the tragedy not just of an ageing thespian, but an entire era, earned him laurels across the country. His poetry inspired freedom fighters during the epic 1942 Quit India movement. Meeting him was an inspiration.

Last night I was standing on a bridge, seeing below
The blazing lights of cars passing by, bright as the burning embers,
I walk on embers every year during Moharrum
Barefoot—
While walking on delicate rose petals
Kusumagraj's feet would be torn by wounds,
And then embers of the freedom struggle would burn brighter

MM Kalburgi

I didn't know him, no ties
Never met him,
Yet, we were kindred souls because of our writing.

He hasn't died
Someone else has
He is right there on the doorstep
Someone rang the doorbell,
He was teaching alphabets to his children
Got up and opened the door

A bullet shrieked... piercing the still air,
The idea always spoke fearlessly
The idea is lying at the doorstep!

Masters

Satyajit Ray

I came to know from Hrishi-da (Hrishikesh Mukherjee) that 'Manik-da wants to meet you.' He was referring to Satyajit Ray. I raced off to Sun-n-Sand, a swanky hotel in suburban Mumbai. I was told that he was in the hotel lawn. As soon as he saw me his baritone voice curled up in the air –'Gulzar?'

He exclaimed, his pronunciation of 'z' in my name was flawless, unlike Bimal-da's.

'Ji, yes...' I said, and pulled up a chair at a respectable distance.

He said, 'I wanted to compliment you. Everyone had told me about you.'

That was my first meeting with Satyajit Ray.

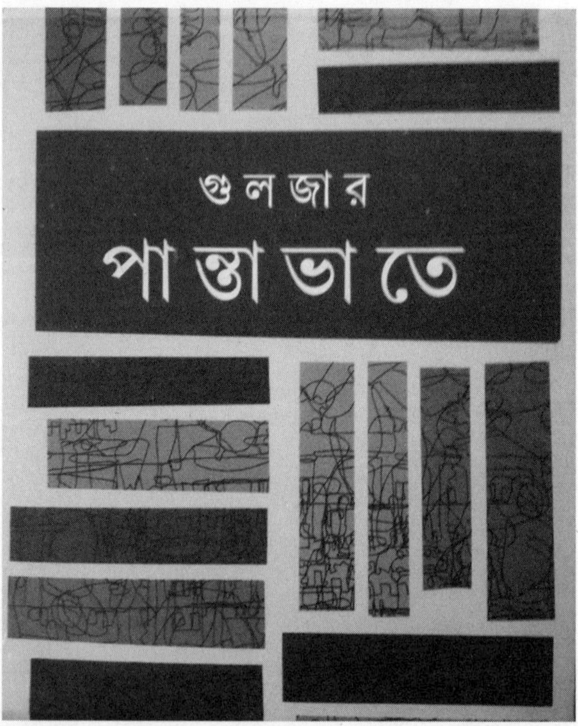

He spoke English like an Englishman! You would have to hear him in order to believe it. Impeccable diction, even his body language reminded you of a 'burra sahib'.

On the other hand, he spoke Bangla like a 'bhadralok' Bengali would. The transformation was amazing. Otherwise, he appeared aloof—a stranger.

To close friends and colleagues, he was Manik-da; I took the cue from them and felt free to use the moniker. He was planning the Hindi version of *Goopy Gyne, Bagha Byne.*

He wanted to discuss with me the script and songs of the Hindi version.

His biggest worry was that the Bengali flavour of the widely acclaimed 1969 film should not be lost in translation. I felt deeply touched that a film-maker of such high calibre was not willing to compromise on the tonal quality and sweetness of his mother tongue.

He asked me if I had watched *Goopy Gyne, Bagha Byne*. I answered in the affirmative.

'Fine, how would you translate "*sadha sidha maatir manush*" into Hindi?'

I sputtered something—whatever came to my mind. 'There isn't much need to change "*sadha sidha*". We can add "*dehati*" to it,' I said. He seemed suitably assured and said 'Good, good' in his baritone. We were there for half an hour.

The meeting came to an end.

Next, I met him in Calcutta (now Kolkata) to discuss the *Goopy Gyne...* script. He asked one of his close aides to get the script, and wrote down the songs for me in Bangla script. He knew I can read Bangla. Given his exalted status anyone would have done the tedious task for him. He, perhaps, was keen that there were no mistakes. This was a lesson for me: how devoted a person can be to his work. His handwritten songs are resting in my treasure chest.

The Hindi version of *Goopy Gyne...* didn't see the light of day; I lost a good opportunity to work with Manik-da. However, we kept in touch. I would often visit the New Theatres studio in connection of my work with Tarun-da—Tarun Majumdar.

Once, I saw Shashi Kapoor, Manik-da and a few others talking among themselves. I stood a little away from them, but I could overhear their conversation. Manik-da was saying—not exactly his words, though—that if we don't have enough funds then we should use our imagination.

One more opportunity came my way. The daughter of Karuna Bandyopadhyay was planning to make an animation serial based on Manik-da's Professor Shanku stories, for Doordarshan. Karuna Bandyopadhyay played the role of Sarbajaya, Apu's mother, in Ray's *Pather Panchali*. I was supposed to do the script which Manik-da was going to vet. I put my heart and soul into the job.

However, we were told that the serial had been put on hold. Ray wanted to re-work it, not using the animation technique, but as live drama. I remarked jokingly that Manik-da had turned down the idea as he didn't like my script.

A few unit members held a different view. They told me that Ray had realised, upon going through my script, that this could be turned into a major production, and that he had deliberately kept the project on hold.

'Well, this is indeed inspiring,' I remarked. However, the cruel fact was that I had lost yet another opportunity.

The third time I went to Manik-da was on my own. I was told that he was to make *Shatranj Ke Khiladi* (1977). I rushed to the hotel only to be told that he had just left for the airport to catch a flight to Calcutta. I took a taxi and reached the airport. In those days, accessing the airport was not a great problem. I caught hold of him. 'Manik-da, I want to work for *Shatranj Ke Khiladi*. I would like to do the Hindi dialogue.'

'You see, I have already asked Shama Zaidi to do the job —the costumes, the designs and things like that. One of those things, you know, Gulzar,' he replied. I was helpless. For days I was sad, sulking.

We remained in touch, but I never got to work with Manik-da. I have a good equation with his son Sandip. I once bumped into him at an international film festival for which he was on the jury panel.

A special screening was to be held the same evening for the jury. I told Sandip that I was keen on seeing the film. 'I shall stand in the projection room. May I see the film?' I asked.

'You can enter from the front. Sit right in the front row. We've often seen films in this manner. Even Baba would do so,' he replied.

Satyajit Ray's appeal was incredible. It enveloped his entire personality. Great sense of cinema, the completeness of a genius, acclaim, personality, devotion, knowledge of the craft and a pinch of childishness—all rolled into a single person.

Is one lifetime enough to get rid of the regret of not having worked with a marvellous person called Satyajit Ray?

Hemanta Mukhopadhyay

A tall Bengali man, draped in a spotless dhoti and shirt, would wander around Mumbai in his Merc. Back in the 1960s, one would hardly see a nonconformist or a prosperous Bengali in Mumbai. This man would sing, score music and produce films too. I am talking about Hemanta-da—Hemanta Kumar. Our dear Hemanta Mukhopadhyay.

I first met Hemanta-da at the recording of '*Ganga aaye kahaan se...*', a song from *Kabuliwala*, Bimal Roy's 1961 film. Hardly had he stepped into the recording room than he lighted a cigarette. He stood before the microphone with a cigarette between his fingers. I was taken aback.

The song was over. I said, 'Hemanta-da, most singers don't smoke as they fear it would kill their voice. And here I see you smoking while recording a song.'

He smiled gently and said, 'If I don't smoke, my voice

doesn't get the right grain. It comes out unclear.' Hemanta-da would never lose his equanimity, rain or sunshine. He was always calm and unruffled.

I can tell you more such amazing stories about Hemanta-da. He was addicted to snuff, and yet his voice was exquisite. He had his own way of taking snuff.

It was an elaborate ritual. He would fish out a small box from his pocket, gently tap it with his thumb. Next, he would hold just a pinch between his thumb and index finger, and then go on talking with those present in the room.

How long can a person hold snuff between his fingers? I often wondered. When will he actually inhale it? Stealing a quick break, he would turn his face away and do the needful.

Next, he would pull out the hem of his dhoti from his pocket and wipe his hands, and stuff the dhoti folds back into his pocket. The entire task was executed with dexterity.

He was grace personified when he held his hands against his chest, à la Swami Vivekananda, during conversations with friends or colleagues.

Tall, ramrod straight, his unique singing style and maverick personality all contributed to his legendary status—a majestic blend which one seldom sees.

We met a few times outside the studio or recording centre. Bimal-da (Bimal Roy) died in 1964. His production house BRP closed down. At this critical hour Hemanta-da came forward and offered work to each of us. A lion of a man, his heart was filled with courage and compassion. He helped us all.

Mukul Dutt, Bimal-da's personal secretary, was a good poet. Hemanta-da asked him to write Bengali songs. He asked me to lend a helping hand to screenplays and write songs for his production house.

Let me tell you how *Khamoshi* happened. We all had gathered, as was the usual practice, at the music room of Hemanta-da's Khar residence. He was fussing over a tune, even as he leaned on a fat pillow. That was how he worked. He would set a song to tune and then sing it aloud.

Suddenly, he asked me, 'Gulzar, tell me, have you seen *Deep Jwele Jaie*?'

'Yes, I have,' I replied, 'But that was long ago. I can't recall the details.'

'How about doing it in Hindi?' he asked.

'Dada, it would be very good,' I replied. Soon, surprisingly, a tapestry of Suchitra Sen's shots from *Deep Jwele Jaie* appeared before my eyes.

'Chalo, let's go,' Dada said and got up.

'Where to?' asked Bela-di, his wife.

Hemanta-da told her that he was going to meet Asit-da—noted director Asit Sen, who had come on a visit to Mumbai. We went to a nearby hotel where Asit-da had checked in.

'Achha Asit, how would you like your *Deep Jwele Jaie* being made in Hindi?' Hemanta-da asked him with his trademark nonchalance.

Asit-da seemed more aloof, even sad. 'Who will make such a film in Hindi?' he asked.

'I am going to do it,' Hemanta-da said, adding, 'Which is why I have come to meet you.'

Asit-da kept silent for a while. Then began an animated discussion on the choice of actors, location, script and so forth.

On our way back, Hemanta-da asked Parimal, his close personal aide, to arrange for a trial show of *Deep Jwele Jaie*.

One has to have a sense of deep conviction and unstinted devotion to art to finalise a film project in flat ten minutes.

Khamoshi is the Hindi version of *Deep Jwele Jaie*. Waheeda-ji was chosen for the lead role. One day Hemanta-da took me along to her residence to discuss the film. That was the first time I saw Waheeda-ji in person.

In *Khamoshi*, I wrote a song. '*Humne dekhi hai un aankhon ki mahekti khushboo...*' Hemanta-da's tune was marvellous.

'Lata will sing the song,' he declared with excitement. Only she can do justice to the melody.

I was aghast. The lover is supposed to sing it to his beloved. 'It would look abundantly odd. A boy should be singing this song,' I said.

Hemanta-da was firm. 'Lata will sing the song,' he reiterated. Finally, Asit Sen hammered out a solution. A woman was shown crooning the number over the radio. Till date, no one has raised any objection, thanks to Hemanta-da's consummate artistry.

'*Humne dekhi hai...*' triggered a minor controversy, though. There was a debate whether I had written a film ditty or a poem. How can hands 'touch' fragrance? However, Hemanta-da was well versed in poetry. He asked me not to pay heed to detractors. 'Gulzar, let people say whatever they want to. Don't change a single line,' he told me. Later, critics made peace with me and coined a term—Gulzaresque—for my imagery.

Did I tell you that Hemanta-da helped me buy a flat, my first home in Mumbai? Yet another story.

Well, I was looking for a house of my own. Shyam, Hemanta-da's assistant, who knew that I was on a house-hunting mission, told me that noted music director Nachiketa Ghosh was looking for a buyer for his north Bombay Society flat at Santacruz, then a beautiful suburb.

'Do you want to buy?' Shyam asked me.

'Are you silly? Where is the money to buy such a big house?' I said.

A day after, Hemanta-da brought up the topic. Shyam had told him everything. 'How can I, Dada? It's pretty difficult for me to buy it,' I said.

'Do one thing, Gulzar,' Hemanta-da said, 'Go tomorrow to

Nachiketa Ghosh and streamline the papers. I have made the down payment.' I was astounded.

Before I could say anything more, he added, 'Don't worry, I'll deduct the money from your remuneration. Which means your job is safe.' Hemanta-da smiled, just a little. I got my first house. My paying guest phase was over.

The house was a small one; it became a meeting place—adda—for friends and comrades because of the bachelor flat-owner's amateurish attempts to make tea. Piles of books and impromptu gatherings of friends lent warmth to the home.

Hemanta-da and Tarun Majumdar would often drop in. Endless cups of tea, books, discussions and soft strains of Rabindra Sangeet would set the mood for the evening.

It so happened that once Hemanta-da, seated on a divan on the floor, was singing Rabindra Sangeet with great vigour. Tanu-da too joined him. However, Hemanta-da couldn't recall a particular line.

Crisis deepened when Tanu-da couldn't come to Hemanta-da's rescue. I was making tea. I spotted Tagore's *Geetobitaan* on the bookshelf, opened the book and, running my finger through the contents, found the song.

Both were amazed. 'You can read Bengali so well?' Hemanta-da asked. I nodded with an impish smile, and went back to stir the tea pot.

Reading Bengali? They would've had the shock of their life to know that I could write Bengali with considerable ease. Actually, I had fallen in love with a Bengali girl (who later became my wife), and exchanged letters with her in Bangla. Hemanta-da knew this, but not about the letters in Bangla.

I soon became addicted to Hemanta-da's Rabindra Sangeet

and other songs. During my frequent visits to Calcutta, I would accompany him to his concerts, and became acquainted with the music scene of Bengal—especially its heartland.

Those were Hemanta-da's salad days. One could say that his fame had occupied a place right next to the sun. He would bring the concert to a grand finale with his soulful, evocative numbers.

There used to be a small tent, next to the pavilion, which served as a resting room for artists. There would be chairs, wooden benches—and tea and biscuits too.

As his predecessors went on stage to perform, Hemanta-da would lie down on a wooden bench and sing Rabindranath's songs, one after the other. Every night I would find myself submerged in divine moments, which, I believed, were created for me.

Hemanta-da was a gem of a man. I had done considerable work on a script for his next venture. Once, I found, on returning home, a note from Hemanta-da, saying that circumstances had compelled him to shelve the project. 'Gulzar, I feel very sorry about this, but there is no way I can go ahead with the film, at least for now,' the note said. I suppose *Faraar*, his latest film, had bombed at the box office.

What a great man! Imagine a successful, charismatic film-maker–singer–music director calling on a junior script writer and lyricist, coming to his house, and not finding him home writes a 'Sorry' note. He could have rung me up—he could just have not informed me at all.

However, Hemanta-da thought I would feel humiliated if I heard from someone about Hemanta-da's decision. His heart melted for a young writer who was fighting his way up. After reading the note, my heart filled with gratitude.

Fortunate me! I thought.

Times began to change in the 1970s. Mumbai was changing at a frenetic pace—and so was the Hindi film industry. Hemanta-da decided to re-locate to Calcutta which, I think, was a right decision. The shifting process went on for years.

Mumbai is ruthless. Hemanta-da perhaps realised that the city may humiliate him. Commerce doesn't tip its hat to creativity.

Calcutta welcomed him with open arms. He earned respect and adulation, which he richly deserved, and a phenomenal following in Bengal.

When he died in Calcutta, he was given a hero's send-off by the people.

Pandit Ravi Shankar

The gentleman who stepped into my room in jeans and a colourful T-shirt and left me speechless was Pandit Ravi Shankar. *The* Ravi Shankar, should I say? It's pointless to use cliches—that he put India on the world map and so forth. Suffice to say that Pandit-ji was the man whose music we grew up with culturally.

A Ravi Shankar-Ustad Ali Akbar Khan 'jugalbandi' was held at the Bharatiya Vidya Bhavan, in south Mumbai, in 1954, to commemorate the birth centenary of Ustad Allaudin Khansaheb, the doyen of the fabled Maihar gharana. I bought a ticket and sat through the night listening to the two stalwarts play with such power and grace. It was later released as a record, which received worldwide acclaim.

I knew him, not from close quarters, though, because of the Indian People's Theatre Association (IPTA), a robust theatre movement which had a nationwide appeal. Pandit-ji had scored music for *Dharti Ke Laal,* produced by IPTA. The entire IPTA team worked with him.

Cut to New York: my first trip to the US of A only to meet Pandit-ji. I was doing *Meera* based on the life of Meerabai, the fourteenth-century saint-poet—and a rebel—from Udaipur. Preparations were underway and we were soon to record songs for the film.

Lata Mangeshkar refused to sing for the film, saying that she had just recorded, with her brother Hridayanath, a non-film album of Meerabai's devotional songs, and that she wouldn't like to sing Meera again. Distressed as I was, I accepted Lata-ji's argument.

Meanwhile, composers Laxmikant-Pyarelal too were dragging their feet. The duo was delaying the recording. It later transpired that L-P were no longer interested in the film as Lata-ji was not going to sing.

Ameen, I said.

Meanwhile, the *Meera* sets were ready and the shoot was to start very soon. Being a dear friend of mine, RD Burman knew that the crown of thorns would now be placed on his head. One day he called up to explain his dilemma. 'With Lata-ji opting out, *Meera*'s songs would go to Asha, which would spark a feud in the family. Gullu, you are my friend, try to understand,' said Pancham.

I was really in a soup. I discussed the matter with producer Prem-ji. He asked me not to worry. 'If the need arises, we will do the sets again, but *Meera* will be done,' he said.

Ameen, again.

After several rounds of hectic discussion, we finalised Pandit-ji's name. Not only was he a great musician but he was above controversies. Hiten Chowdhury, who was Prem-ji's friend, knew Kamala Shankar. She was close to him, and would often accompany him on the tanpura in concerts. Moreover, she planned his concerts in India. Hiten-da rang her up. She said Pandit-ji was in the US, and that we could put him a call.

Hiten-da promptly rang up Pandit-ji. He said he would do *Meera* if he liked the script. I felt a bit confident and told Prem-ji that I would like to talk to Pandit-ji.

'Go ahead,' Prem-ji said.

I rang up Pandit-ji. The reply came from the other end in a velvet voice: 'I'll do the film if I like the script. You can send it to me.'

'What if I come there and read the script to you?' I asked. A moment's pause. 'You want to come here, to New York?' he asked.

'Yes,' I said.

'Fine, you can come. I'll make lodging and other arrangements for you,' Pandit-ji said.

Prem-ji asked me not to go alone. 'Take Hiten-da with you. You don't know him well enough,' he said. Thus, I set out on my maiden visit to the US. From the airport we drove straight to the hotel. The doorbell rang at around 4 p.m., and, to our utter surprise, Pandit-ji stood before us, in jeans and a colourful tee-shirt. A middle-aged gentleman, looking smart, glowing with youth.

I had never thought that Pandit-ji would come to meet us in person. It was decided that I should go to his place the following day for a script session. 'What is this controversy about Lata-ji? I don't want to get into any row,' he said, adding that he wished to talk to Lata-ji.

Lata-ji was in Washington in connection with a concert tour. I rang her up and told her that Pandit-ji wanted to speak to her. 'I'll certainly talk to him if he calls,' she replied. Renowned playback singer Mukesh too had joined Lata-ji's tour, and I spoke briefly with him—my last conversation with him as he died in the middle of the tour. This was in August 1976.

My dilemma was how to tell Pandit-ji that Lata-ji wanted

him to ring her up. I was nervous. Eventually, I gathered courage and told him so in a soft, respectful tone, peppering my conversation with lots of *kintu*—but.

'That's fine,' Ravi-da said, 'I will call her.' Nothing is impossible if you are honest to your work.

It was decided that Pandit-ji would, in the intervening period, do dummy songs. He said he would snatch time amidst a hectic concert schedule to work on some songs, the rest would be wrapped up in September during his visit to India.

My heart sank. 'But Dada, I want to record the songs in September,' I said, my voice quivering with fear.

'How is it possible? Even if I set the songs to tune you will have to sit with me,' he said.

'Suppose I join you on your tour. You can do the songs in the spare time—I am going to be with you,' I said.

Ravi-da looked at me and smiled—and then laughed heartily. '*Chhokre*, you are adamant,' he remarked.

I accompanied Pandit-ji to London where we worked on songs. From London I returned to Mumbai via Amsterdam, and I was starstruck. Many ace musicians participated in the dusk-to-dawn concert. Pandit-ji's recital got off to a dazzling start a little before midnight. I could see the night evolving, mutating from black to cobalt blue, and then it deepened, suffused with some mysterious shade of black. It was mesmerising.

The dawn broke majestically through the church panels, Pandit-ji's Raag Bhairavi was serenading the first rays of the sun just as it had caressed the deep blue night. The delicate fragrance of Raag Bhairavi was floating in the air. I remembered the young, vivacious sitarist with curly hair who had taken Woodstock by storm way back in 1969. In Amsterdam, Pandit-ji's lily-fresh musical notes shaped the idea of morning. Perhaps, God looks like him, I thought.

From London, I and my colleagues returned to Mumbai, while Pandit-ji went back to New York. He said, 'Gulzar, there won't be any problem. We can record the songs in September.' Taking him at his word, we got down to work with renewed fervour.

However, a thought kept throbbing at the back of my mind: If Lata didi and Asha-ji are not going to sing, whose voice will Pandit-ji choose? He asked me if I was fine with Vani Jayaram. 'Any objections? I was on cloud nine. 'What objection can I raise and why? It was I who wrote Vani-ji's debut film song—"*Bol re papeehara...*" from *Guddi*,' I said.

'That's right,' said Pandit-ji, 'I want a voice adequately trained in classical music which can act as a backdrop to the new interpretation, set to classical tunes, of Meera's bhajans. Vani can do this.'

I was excited like a child. Meera had captured my imagination. Pandit-ji arrived in Mumbai in September. The rest of the songs were ready. We got going with the recordings—a gruelling, twelve-hour shift between 9 a.m. and 9 p.m. Soft strains of divine music filled the air. It seemed as if we were enveloped in a dream. Fact blended seamlessly with fantasy.

Everything was going as per the schedule. Pandit-ji was conducting rehearsals, songs were being recorded, mistakes were being corrected—but something was missing. Pandit-ji seemed a bit upset.

On the fourth day after we had wrapped up yet another song, Pandit-ji said, 'Tell me, can we have the recording tomorrow at two in the afternoon?'

'No problem,' I replied. I didn't feel like asking him why. He may have his own reasons, I thought.

Next day Pandit-ji arrived at the studio at 2 p.m. sharp. He looked fresh and the recording studio became a happy place, his infectious smile lighting up the studio. After a while he called me and said, 'You know, I didn't touch my sitar for the last four days. When I don't follow my riyaz schedule I feel uneasy—as if something has remained undone, incomplete. I am feeling better today as I practised from four in the morning till twelve noon. Without riyaz I feel emaciated. Now I am fine. Let's get back to our dear Giridhar Gopal.'

I was astonished. I realised that sadhana—unalloyed, pure devotion—is a physical thing. The body is in pain when you don't follow the *riyaz* regimen. The body is our biggest teacher, the most powerful medium. This can't be explained or taught. It has to be experienced, felt and understood.

The recordings were over, the record was released. *Meera*, my dream, my contemplation, was there on the silver screen. We remained in touch, but our meetings were few and far between. We once met in Agra; Anushka, Pandit-ji's daughter, was a child. Also, it was my first meeting with his wife Sukanya.

The meeting is deeply etched in my mind for a reason which can be described as strange and amusing. It was essentially a pleasant talk and the atmosphere was informal. Suddenly, Sukanya asked me, 'Don't I look a bit like Rakhee-ji?'

I was hugely embarrassed. The answer was beyond my imagination. I may play with words, sentences and languages, but I realised that I was yet to acquire the craft to give a smart reply to a question such as this. I mumbled something to the effect that they both were beautiful in different ways and that it was a tad difficult to comment on the subject.

However, I found a puckish smile playing on Pandit-ji's lips. I didn't try to decode it.

Pandit Bhimsen Joshi

I wouldn't claim that I understand the subtleties of Indian classical music, but I realised long ago that it has a sensuous appeal. I am mesmerised by Pandit Ravi Shankar's sitar, Ustad Amjad Ali's sarod and Pandit Bhimsen Joshi's gayaki.

Just that the classical singer's facial expressions and movements of hands strike a discordant note. I don't like tennis star Rafael Nadal just because he runs his thumb and finger down his nose too often.

The only exception is Pandit Bhimsen Joshi. He does frantic movements of hands and his facial muscles contort too, but when he sings it seems he has held a musical note by the neck and is trying to drag it down; or, he has been giving a dressing down following which the sur obeys his orders like an obedient school boy, and blends seamlessly with his vocal chords.

Timber is the unique quality of Pandit Joshi's voice. Also, I was floored by the sheer energy in his gayaki. I used to have a heap of Pandit-ji's cassettes in my car; but I can't analyse his music. I only know that hearing him sing is akin to taking a dip in the cool waters of a placid pond.

A friend of mine, Dr Kishan Morwani, from the tennis court, would celebrate his son's birthday every year on 10 October with Pandit-ji's concert at his residence. We would all get the opportunity to hear Pandit-ji to our heart's content.

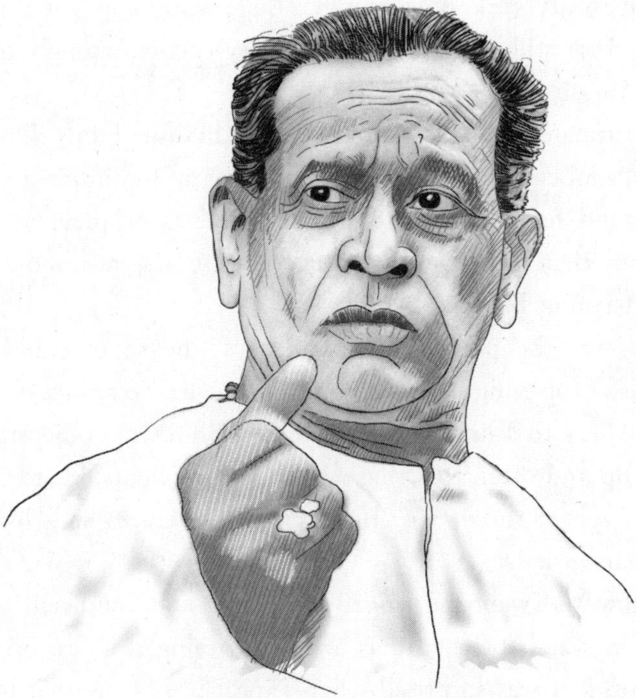

It so happened that Vinod Khanna once decided to skip a noisy, glitzy party on his birthday and instead hosted Pandit-ji's concert at his residence. Vinod forced me to sit in the front. I was embarrassed. Why should I sit before such a great artist? I thought. In front of me sat film-maker Raj Khosla.

No sooner had Pandit-ji begun to sing than I saw Khosla nodding his head and shouting waah-waahs. This went on for quite some time. Suddenly, Pandit-ji stopped in the middle of a dazzling alaapi and, addressing Khosla, said, 'Sir, you are uttering waah-waah even before I've made a shot outside the boundary. You better sit a little behind and you (he pointed at me) come up front.'

My heart sank. Given my meagre knowledge of classical music, I sat still and motionless lest my encore, wrongly timed, upset Pandit-ji.

Fortunately, I was commissioned by the Films Division to do a documentary on Pandit Bhimsen Joshi. He is from Pune, and had a troublesome childhood as he grew up with a stepmother. However, a music shop in the neighbourhood altered young Bhimsen's life.

As was the practice in those days, the shop would play records of top-rung singers all through the day to attract patrons. On his way to school and back home, Bhimsen would stop by the shop and listen to Ustad Abdul Karim Khan's records, who was a rage in the 1930s. Bhimsen would try to sing like the legendary ustad.

How the wannabe singer left home and wandered across India in search of a guru is a heartwarming story of grit and hard work. I was surprised when Pandit-ji told me that he ran away from home because his stepmother would discriminate between him and her own son while applying ghee to freshly roasted rotis. She would put more ghee on her son's rotis. 'You actually left home because of that?' I asked.

'No,' he replied with a chuckle. 'That was just an excuse. In those days young boys had to run away from home to learn music or join a drama company,' he said. 'I wanted to learn music, come what may.'

Bhimsen-ji had heard of Ustad Hafiz Ali Khan. A great sarod player (and father of Ustad Amjad Ali Khan), Ustad Hafiz Ali was the presiding deity of Gwalior, which was one of the leading centres of classical music.

Bhimsen-ji boarded a long-distance train, ticketless and

penniless. The ticket checker had neither the time nor the inclination to admire the creative urge of an eleven-year-old wannabe singer. As the boy had no money to pay the fine, he was clapped in jail.

Out of prison, Bhimsen-ji, unfazed, continued his journey—travelling ticketless, going hungry, sleeping on streets and railway platforms, and playing hide and seek with burly ticket checkers. Two months later he was in Gwalior, the city of his dreams.

Looking back on those years, Pandit-ji said, 'If I came across a connoisseur, I would literally force him to listen to Ustad Abdul Karim's composition—in my voice! Often, a ticket checker would enjoy my music and then pack me off to the railway lock-up.'

Bhimsen sang before Ustad Hafiz Ali. The ustad was astonished. Such bright possibilities in a voice so young and tender, he thought. He got Bhimsen-ji enrolled in the famous Scindia School. However, the boy found comfort not in learning but riyaz, which he never skipped. Quitting Scindia School was not a viable option as students were entitled to free lunch.

At night, Bhimsen-ji would keep pottering around Ustad Hafiz Ali's house. A lion of a man, the ustad would ask the pupil to join him for dinner. Ustad Hafiz Ali had an eagle's eye, he knew Bhimsen was talented. Not for nothing did he teach Raag Darbari Kanada, a majestic, multi-layered raag, to the young student.

Having spent two years in Gwalior, Bhimsen-ji fled to Calcutta to be the disciple of Bhishmadev Chattopadhyay, who was revered as the god of music. There was no way he could have gained access to Bhishmadev Babu's residence. Bhimsen-ji came know that Bhishmadev Babu taught music to Pahari Sanyal, the renowned actor-singer of Bengal, at the latter's residence.

Bhimsen-ji managed to get a job in Sanyal Babu's kitchen! He used to cook food and carry the lunch box to the studio every day—and learn music on the sly. Bengalis would be shocked to read this.

After spending two years at Pahari Sanyal's bungalow as a cook, Bhimsen trekked to Jalandhar. A well-known centre of classical music, Jalandhar used to host the prestigious Harballabh Sangeet Sammelan every year, in which the titans of music participated with great pride. Bhimsen-ji learnt music from a visually impaired guru for nearly two years. The kind-hearted guru made arrangements with a local restaurant for Bhimsen-ji's lunch and dinner.

Pandit Bhimsen was deeply moved when he heard Sawai Gandharva sing at the Harballabh conference. Sawai Gandharva belonged to Dharwar which was near Pune, where Bhimsen-ji lived.

Eventually, the long quest for the guru ended, and Bhimsen-ji became the 'ganda-bandh' pupil (a ritual which sanctifies the guru-shishya relationship) of Sawai Gandharva. The training was rigorous. He lived with the guru, cooked meals for him, cleaned the house and drew water from a nearby well.

Recalling his formative years, he once said, 'I remember someone. When I used to go to fetch water for my guru's bath, a woman would keep looking at me. Later, she would stop me on my way and offer me a glass of milk. How strange, isn't it?'

After he was through with his training, Pandit-ji came to Mumbai. He used to sing for All India Radio. Soon, the iconic HMV company released his records, which won him critical acclaim. The rest, as they say, is history.

Pandit-ji carries his greatness with amazing grace and child-like vulnerability. He was once telling me how senior he was in the field of music. He said, 'Bachha (son), I first heard Begum Akhtar when she used to be standing while rendering a thumri or a dadra.'

'But why did she have to stand and sing?' I asked.

'Decades ago, artists would get a chance to sing but they were asked to stand. After they proved their mettle, they were allowed to sit with accompanists and sing. I have known Akhtaribai since those times,' he added.

Bhimsen-ji was in Calcutta for a concert. Pahari Sanyal was seated in the front row. After the concert was over, Pandit-ji walked up to Pahari Babu and told him that he was the same Joshi who, years ago, used to work in his kitchen. Pahari Babu was stumped—he couldn't utter a word. The teenaged boy who used to bring his lunch box to the studio was now a doyen of classical music. Pandit-ji could never forget the expression on the thespian's face.

Pandit-ji had a passion for cars. An accomplished driver, he would travel to Mangalore and Bangalore in his Merc. He would often drive himself to concerts in distant towns.

I once went to him in the morning. He was feasting on roti and pickle. I was taken aback. I said, 'Why would you be eating pickle? I've heard that singers keep away from oily, hot things.' His answer summed up his sadhana, his commitment to music. 'I have been doing riyaz for so many years now that my voice has solidified into a block of dry wood. Nothing will harm my vocal chords.'

Such mind-boggling creativity and such endearing

innocence—like a child Bholenath. Can an artist achieve greatness without contradictions?

Salil Chowdhury

Salil Chowdhury was like a bottle of champagne which, when shaken vigorously and uncorked, releases drunkenness and joi de vivre. His vivacity would touch our lives and melt in our blood—like light which spreads its glow everywhere.

I knew Salil-da much before I came into films, thanks to the Indian People's Theatre Association (IPTA) and the Bombay Youth Choir (BYC). Back in the 1960s, Salil-da was a firebrand Communist activist and lyricist. His songs were popular and often attracted state ban.

Salil-da would either be in jail or go 'underground'. I was floored by the magic and mystique of his personality, his impeccable creative skills.

Singer-actor Ruma (Guhathakurta) had flagged off the BYC with Salil-da as her senior, much-respected colleague and mentor.

He would write and compose songs, conduct rehearsals, take the IPTA-BYC team on tours. Those were the days when poverty would co-exist with poetry—tears with tiaras. Salil-da and I would wander around Mumbai's slums on a sunny afternoon.

On knowing him closely I realised that Salil-da is a first-class work shirker—busy playing carrom, ping-pong or table tennis. He would be doing everything except his work. But music would flow like a river of nectar when his fingers danced, with the sublime grace of a Russian ballerina, on the piano or the harmonium.

Why should a genius live with such contradictions? Or, well, why not? Only a genius can afford such a luxury, I suppose.

Such excellence, mindfulness of a mendicant, contemplation gushing like a waterfall; robust creativity, such vitality and restlessness.

Salil-da would spend the entire day playing carrom at Mohan Studios. For him, carrom was of paramount importance. Why should anyone bother him with songs?

Salil-da was once playing carrom. A colleague came and said that a Chrysler was up for sale.

'I don't want,' Salil-da said.

'Never mind, but take a look at the car once.'

'I don't want, yaar. Let me play,' Salil-da was hopelessly engrossed in the game.

'Dada, available on easy instalments.'

He bought it.

A funny story about Salil-da used to do the rounds. If someone brought an elephant for him, he would calmly reply, '*Mujhe nahin chahiye* (I don't want).' If the person persisted, 'On instalments, Dada.' Salil-da without taking his eyes off the 'queen', would say, 'OK, tie the elephant in the courtyard.'

Salil-da was never in need of money; he earned well. It's just that he was a big spender.

Making Salil-da work on songs was a tough task; he would do everything, except his assignment as composer. Try telling him, 'Salil-da, you were to do that song, no?' and he would brush off the idea with a wave of a hand, saying, 'That, of course, will happen...don't worry. Look, I've got this new car, let's go on a drive to Powai. We'll have a trial run as well.' He was fond of cars.

The tune would be tossed out of the window and they would

zoom off to the idyllic Powai hamlet in suburban Mumbai. The *Kabuliwala* shooting was on. I, Balraj Sahni and one of Bimal-da's assistants were off to Calcutta to shoot the film's title shots with Kamal Bose, the cameramen.

When we returned, Bimal-da told me, 'Two songs have been recorded, Goljar...go hear them.' 'Goljar' was Bimal-da's version of my name—in impeccable Bengali! I told Bimal-da that I didn't much like the bhajan.

'Hmmm,' was Bimal-da's trademark reply. He then asked me to sit with Salil-da to replace the song tune. Who was going to write the song? Prem Dhawan had penned the other numbers of *Kabuliwala*. How can I? Unethical! I thought.

A bit disconcerted, I went to Salil-da.

'Prem Dhawan has told Bimal-da that Gulzar will write the song.'

Salil-da told me.

'Prem had to go on a tour with the IPTA team; he suggested your name so that Bimal-da doesn't upset his tour plan,' Salil-da added.

Eventually I agreed, but where was the tune? Bimal-da asked me twice or thrice; each time I mumbled something—'You know, Salil-da doesn't have enough time.' Some gobbledygook!

Meanwhile, Rajan Tarafdar's *Ganga*, a Bengali film, was released. I liked the song '*Amai dubaili re...*' from the film. A few days later, I went to Salil-da's house. Salil-da was playing table tennis downstairs. I asked him if the song could be set to the tune of '*Amai dubaili re...*'

Salil-da was miffed—I had ruined his game. 'OK, go up, sit with Kanu and do the song,' he said. I met Kanu, Salil-da's assistant, and we both sat down to work.

Suddenly, we heard the honking of a station wagon. Bimal-da had arrived. Salil-da raced up the staircase in a jiffy like a school brat and sat down to play the piano pretending as if he had been immersed in the tune for ages! He knew that Bimal-da was standing at the door. However, he pretended as if he was unmindful of the world around him.

In a well-studied move, he 'saw' Bimal-da and said, 'Oh, Bimal-da, you know I am wondering if the tune of "*Amai dubaili re*" can be transferred to the *Kabuliwala* song.' Saying this he closed his eyes and began to run his fingers on the keyboard with the passion of a rugby player. Bimal-da was at the door. 'Just a thought that crossed my mind, you know,' Salil-da added solicitously.

Bimal-da said, 'You don't have to think so hard when you are drowning, Salil. Just do the song,' said Bimal-da and walked away looking abundantly annoyed.

Hardly had his car left, when Salil-da jumped from his seat and rushed back to his table tennis game but not before admonishing me like a cranky school master, 'Listen Gulzar, you can go only after finishing the task with Kanu.' As if I was not letting him work. He was back to his table tennis. What could I say?

The *Kabuliwala* song was '*Ganga aaye kahan se...*'

Salil Chowdhury was like a Tsunami in the ocean of creativity, gushing down with a blazing force, eternal joy and playfulness.

Mighty, magnificent and magical.

Sippy Sahab—Mere Apne

Imagine a top-heavy producer summoning a thirty-something writer home at 4 a.m. to discuss a film project over ginger tea! Thus began the journey of *Mere Apne*, my first film as director, way back in 1970.

Producer NC Sippy was made from a different cloth. He stood ramrod straight in the world of fleeting images, fragile friendships and fluctuating fortunes—head and shoulders above his peers.

The story of how *Mere Apne* was made would make a captivating film script. The film was adapted from Tapan Sinha's *Apan Jan*, a stark film with an old woman as the central protagonist.

A distant nephew seeks out the hapless 'bua' (aunt), who is quietly spending her sunset years in a village, and brings her to Calcutta (now Kolkata) with a promise that she would be looked after well by him and his wife.

However, the old lady is soon reduced to a domestic help and is subjected to humiliation. Thrown out of the house, she befriends a beggar child, and a group of jobless youths from the neighbourhood.

Based on a short story by Indra Mitra, *Apan Jan* skilfully fused Anandi Bua's plight with the country's burgeoning socio-political crisis. Unbridled corruption, shortage of essential commodities, inflation, unemployment and decline in values had made Young India restless and helpless.

Calcutta witnessed street violence, and the rise of rough and ready politics and naxalism. Morchas and bandhs were rampant. Tapan-da tackled the urban themes of loneliness and violence with sensitivity. Chhaya Devi, the fabulously talented actor of Bengali cinema, portrayed the old woman with immaculate grace.

Preparations were soon underway for the Hindi version. Tapan-da summoned me to Calcutta to write the script, which, actually, was the Hindi adaptation of the original Bengali.

However, things didn't go well right from the word go. Producer Ravindranath Malhotra, despite his love for Bengal and its effervescent culture, was eager to turn the Hindi version into a commercial potboiler. He wanted to replace Chhaya Devi with Waheeda Rehman and add to the film two dance numbers picturized on her to make the cash registers jingle at the box office. Hindi filmdom's appetite for profit is monstrous.

Tapan-da quit the project. I returned to Mumbai.

A few days later I met Sippy Sahab. On knowing that I had just returned from Calcutta, he began talking about *Apan Jan*. He wanted to know if I had the film's rights. I didn't, and told him so. 'But I know for sure that Tapan-da is not going to direct the Hindi version.' I then briefly recounted the story to him.

'See if we can get the rights from Malhotra,' he said and left.

It so happened that I met Sippy Sahab again, this time at Mohan Studio where Hrishi-da (Hrishikesh Mukherjee) was shooting his next film. As Sippy Sahab was about to leave, I accompanied him to his car, a Fiat.

'If Hrishi-da is not going to do the Hindi version I would like to do it,' I told Sippy Sahab.

'Do you have the script?' he asked.

'Yes,' I replied.

'Come home tomorrow at 4 a.m.,' he said and the Fiat zoomed off.

The next day I was at Sippy Sahab's doorstep at the appointed hour. Mumbai was in deep slumber, the first suburban train may have chugged out of the iconic Churchgate station, and milkmen were out on the road with their cycles and tin cans.

Sippy Sahab made tea for both of us.

'Who will be your actors?' Sippy Sahab asked. The question scarcely suggested that I was going to direct the film. I said Chhaya Devi was best suited for bua's role. 'She speaks Hindi very well,' I added.

Cutting me in Sippy Sahab asked me to think of a Hindi film star. He wanted Nimmi-ji on board, while I was keen on signing up Meena Kumari-ji.

'It would be nice if you can rope in Nimmi-ji. I had a crush on her,' he chuckled.

'The film will crash at the box office because of your crush,' I remarked jokingly. We both laughed heartily.

'Who will talk to Meena-ji? You or me?' he asked.

Wow!

This was a clear indication that I was going to direct the film. My face lit up. Sippy Sahab must have noticed it. He said, 'Gulzar, I made up my mind last evening when you came to see me off at the parking lot. Calling you home today at 4 a.m. wasn't your test. But it certainly showed your eagerness, your will to make the film. That matters a lot.' His partner may not like an outsider as a director on their banner.

Sippy Sahab was going to talk to Meena-ji—especially, about her remuneration. I would later brief her about the role, I said. Sippy Sahab made it clear that he didn't want to be involved with the film as producer.

Instead, he asked his sons—Romu and Raj (Daddu)—to handle *Mere Apne*. The film was supposed to be an Uttam Chitra production, one more banner of Sippy Sahab. He asked me not to mention his name to anyone. 'You, Romu and Raj should stir the broth, leave me out,' he remarked.

Actually, Sippy Sahab didn't want Hrishi-da to know about *Mere Apne*. Both had a long association going back to the 1960s. Sippy Sahab gave an evasive answer when Hrishi-da asked him. 'I don't know what these boys are doing; I gave them my banner,' he replied casually.

Nevertheless, Sippy Sahab's name appears in the credit titles of *Mere Apne*—'Presented by NC Sippy.'

I owed him as much.

Sippy Sahab was keen that his sons should work as my ADs. However, Romu stuck to production. 'That's my métier,' he said. He later turned out to be a very good producer. Like father, like son. Quiet and firm.

Sippy Sahab took quick decisions; no hemming and hawing. When I told him that I wanted Vinod Khanna to play one of the two principal protagonists in *Mere Apne*—the other being Shatrughan Sinha—Sippy Sahab wanted to see Khanna on the silver screen. We went to Imperial Cinema in south Bombay to watch Khanna's *Mera Gaon Mera Desh*. We left post-interval.

'We'll talk to Vinod,' Sippy Sahab said. That's that.

Shatrughan, who was in regular contact with Sippy Sahab, soon joined us. So did Danny Denzongpa and Dinesh Thakur. All newcomers, a few from FTII, Pune.

Subhash Ghai dropped out—by choice. Both he and Asrani met me. I had one last role in my bag. Ghai recommended Asrani's name. Years later, Ghai told me that he had made up his mind that he would direct films.

Mere Apne had four songs in all; all were recorded, but only two made the cut: *'Koiee hota jisko apna'* and *'Haalchaal theek thaak hai'*.

'Roz akeyli aaye, roz akeyli jaaye' was dropped in view of Meena-ji's deteriorating health.

In the song I have described the moon as the beggar's bowl —*'chand katora'*. Many protested. Meena-ji asked me not to get perturbed by criticism. 'You are a poet; if you think the moon looks like a beggar's bowl, you will write accordingly. Don't worry about what others say.' But she loved the image.

'Ganga...ganga ki bhari goad mein', a boatman's song sung by Manna Dey, was set aside as well.

I have made liberal use of visuals—film posters, ad hoardings and graffitis—to comment on topical issues. For instance, graffitis, which depict the 1971 Bangladesh carnage, can be seen during the song *'Haalchaal theek thaak hai'*.

Two mishaps, in quick succession, left me shattered. First, a set depicting a bazaar came down crashing because of heavy rains. It was built on an open ground. A few days later, a huge fire gutted the entire studio floor, including a set showing Meena-ji's village home.

Sippy Sahab rushed to the studio, and from there drove to my house. I couldn't figure out why on earth would he come to see me so early in the morning in his pyjamas and shirt?

He asked for cold beer.

'Bhaisahab, I don't keep beer,' I said.

'Arrey, a film-maker without cold beer in the fridge? OK, get me some tea.'

He then asked me tactfully if we could shift the set to another studio—say, for instance, Rajkamal in Parel. 'There are labour problems in Mohan Studio,' he said, his eyes trying to tap my response just in case he told me the truth.

Eventually, he did.

'The entire set has been destroyed,' he added. I was shell-shocked. I told Sippy Sahab that I wanted to visit the set. Now, immediately.

We both drove to Mohan Studio. The place was in a mess: clouds of smoke and ash strewn all over. I had tears in my eyes.

However, Sippy Sahab handled the crisis with courage and calm. Never did he lose his cool nor did he pay attention to so-called well-wishers who advised him to disband the project as the director was a novice. After the fire episode some people told him that nature too was not in favour of the film!

Sippy Sahab was unfazed. I tip my hat to him.

Achanak was a breeze. Khwaja Ahmed Abbas's story, which had appeared in *Imprint*, a literary magazine of considerable repute, was short and crisp. The film couldn't have gone beyond ninety minutes flat. Sippy Sahab was ready to back *Achanak*. 'Keep the film tight and sharp, no songs. Like foreign films, which begin after the interval,' he said.

I read out the script to Sippy Sahab at his house—at four in the morning, while his family was busy with preparations for Romu's marriage!

We had to secure rights from Abbas Sahab. A couple of days later, we went to see him. Abbas Sahab was Sippy Sahab's neighbour in Juhu.

We were told that Abbas Sahab had just left for the airport to catch a flight to Delhi. We rushed to the airport. Abbas Sahab was a bit surprised to see us. I told him about the film. 'We'll talk after I return from Delhi. I will give you the original story in Urdu,' he said.

I told Abbas Sahab that Sippy Sahab was the film's producer. Both shook hands. Sippy Sahab quietly pushed an envelope into Abbas Sahab's hand—the signing amount. Didn't this all happen '*achanak*?' Abbas Sahab was surprised.

Koshish was my third film, in a row, with Sippy Sahab. He liked the story of a differently abled couple, both of whom could neither hear nor speak. I was inspired by *Happiness of Us Alone*, noted Japanese director Zenjo Matsuyama's 1961 film—a story of a couple that suffers from loss of hearing, trying to come to terms with post-war society.

Matsuyama apparently believed that differently abled persons need to be pulled out of the mainstream to safeguard their dignity. I took a different view. To me this was segregation and hence reactionary. A differently abled person can certainly re-affirm his/her identity by being part of the mainstream, and function within the framework of societal values. I added a blind man's character in it to prove my point.

Sippy Sahab was willing to back me, while Romu and Daddu took a dim view of the film. However, I couldn't agree with Sippy Sahab's suggestion that the film should have sub-titles. True that the two central protagonists were not going to speak in the film, but that wasn't going to harm the style or substance of *Koshish*. Also, other characters were going to speak in the film, I argued.

We had several rounds of discussions. Finally, Sippy Sahab sought a word of advice from producer-director Chetan Anand, poet Kaifi Azmi and music director Madan Mohan. All three rubbished the idea of *Koshish*.

'Doing a silent film is like turning back Time's wheel,' they declared unanimously. Sippy Sahab seemed keen to go by their verdict. I was adamant on mine.

Meanwhile, I started work on *Parichay* for another production house. Yet, *Koshish* was humming at the back of my mind. Few months later, I met Sippy Sahab and brought up the topic. If he was not interested in *Koshish*, could I start talks with other producers? By then I had gained a bit of confidence.

Sippy Sahab was miffed. 'What's wrong with you, Gulzar? Three senior people from the industry have said that the script doesn't lend itself to film. I say, how adamant are you!'

'Bhaisahab, let me try. Two characters won't speak, but I have music, lighting, cinematography, and a whole lot of supporting characters. If I fail to convey the story then I am not a good director.'

Sippy Sahab ordered tea for both of us; we talked of other things for a while. As I was about to leave, Sippy Sahab asked Romu to give me a cheque—my signing amount for *Koshish*!

'I know that you both and Gulzar are not on the same page as far as *Koshish* is concerned, but I will back him. He seems firm; let me see what he does with the script,' he told Romu.

I was left speechless.

Khoobsurat was my next film with Sippy Sahab. Hrishi-da was the director. He asked me to suggest a name for the untitled film. I suggested *Namkeen.* Hrishi-da liked it, but two days later asked for another title. Sippy Sahab remarked jokingly that Hrishi-da should present me a bottle of cognac as remuneration. I suggested *Khoobsurat*, which was promptly accepted by both. I got my *Namkeen* back from Hrishi-da, and a bottle of cognac too!

I was fortunate that I could work with Sippy Sahab. He was a lion of a man. Underneath the tough exterior lurked a noble soul—and that made all the difference.

Sahir and Jadu

This happened a little before Sahir's funeral.

Actually, the story I am about to recount belon to Jadu, but it has Sahir Ludhianvi's name engraved on it.

Jadu is Javed Akhtar's monicker—his, as they say, pet name. He and his entire family has been weaned on poetry. Jadu's father was Jan Nisar Akhtar; poet Majaz was his maternal uncle, and Kaifi Azmi, his father-in-law. As a callow youth, Jadu was a first-class rebel.

Jadu never got along with his father. In fact, he was full of resentment for Jan Nisar Akhtar. After his mother died Javed could take it no more; he would often leave home and go straight to Sahir.

Both had an excellent equation.

A cursory glance at Jadu and Sahir would make one realise that the boy has had a terrible fight with Jan Nisar Akhtar, who was a close friend of Sahir.

Sahir dare not ask a question; he knew Jadu would blow his top and the high drama would end with the latter's sobs and tears. Too messy for Sahir to handle.

After moments of pregnant silence, Sahir would break the ice, saying, 'Come Jadu, let's sit down for breakfast.' This would prompt Jadu to bare his heart; he would spend the entire day with his host.

Often, Sahir would forewarn Jadu, 'Look, Akhtar is going to be here for lunch.' Jadu would look up with disgust, his eyebrows arched, as if he wanted to tell Sahir, 'Good lord, this man called Akhtar would not leave me alone even in your house.'

If possible, he would have further added, 'Why should this misfortune keep shadowing me every hour of my life?'

Jadu was more like Majaz—sensitive to a fault and reeking

of anger. All those years Sahir indulged Jadu, and soothed his ruffled feathers with both tact and affection.

Sahir would say, 'Jadu, Eros is showing a nice movie, yaar. I can't recall the name... Go and watch it.' Nice way to avert father-son showdown should Akhtar arrive on the scene.

Once, Jadu, in a fit of rage, walked out of Sahir's apartment, saying, 'You have indulged my father for no rhyme or reason.'

Sahir smiled indulgently.

Jadu retorted, 'My "baap" (father) too laughs at me. I want no one; neither my father, nor you...' And he stormed out of Sahir's home.

Jadu remained untraceable for a few days. Attitude or bloated self-esteem—whatever you may call it. Jadu was not the one to yield. Chin up, he held his head high. Where did he eat? Where did he sleep? Who knows?

Meanwhile, Jadu had forged a friendship with the production manager of renowned film-maker-writer Kamal Amrohi. He would spend the evening with him, and sleep in the studio's damp, dust-filled storehouse, which was chock-a-block with all kinds of furniture, props and memorabilia, including two *Filmfare* trophies of Meena Kumari.

And a life-size mirror.

Jadu would do a quick jig before the mirror: he would present the *Filmfare* trophy to himself and, in a jiffy, he would be its recipient! And then he would clap and bow gently to the glittering audience.

Years later, Javed himself recounted the story and added, 'I would rehearse the *Filmfare* episode almost every day before going off to sleep.' He stayed in the studio for several days.

One day he was back at Sahir's suburban apartment—looking

pale, face pulled down. Sahir-ji greeted him with affection. As if nothing had happened. However, Jadu was sulking.

'I am going to use your toilet, I need your soap,' he said.

Sahir-ji nodded in approval. 'Eat something,' he said after a well-scrubbed Jadu stepped out of the toilet.

'I'll eat anywhere...not in your house.'

Sahir placed a hundred rupee note on the dressing table, but didn't know how to cajole Jadu to accept it. He was aware of his young friend's heightened sense of self-respect. 'Jadu, keep this money with you. I'll take it back from you,' Sahir said, a tad cagily. Back then, hundred rupees was a big amount. One had to go to a bank or petrol pump for change.

Javed took the crisp note from Sahir with condescension—as if he was doing a great favour to his senior comrade.

It so happened that Javed began to work with producer-director Shankar Mukherjee. There he met Salim Khan. In no time Javed began to earn very well. He would hit the bottle with vengeance just as his 'Mama' did, and vent his spleen on his father. For whatever reasons, he never bothered to repay Sahir's debt.

In later years, Javed earned in lakhs, but he would tell Sahir, tongue firmly in cheek, 'I've swallowed your hundred rupees.' And Sahir would retort with a laugh, 'Beta, I will make you cough it up for me.' Needless to say, the friendship deepened with each passing year.

Sahir had a small circle of friends. They would all meet every evening, uncork a bottle, crack jokes, eat sumptuous food—and with each peg lambast their rivals in strongest, even abusive language. And laugh.

I can recall one such evening. Sahir was staying in writer

Krishna Chandra's building. Omprakash Ashk, Sahir's long-time friend, asked the poet in chaste Punjabi, 'Sahir, what makes you so abusive after a few pegs down?'

Sahir's reply too was in impeccable Punjabi, 'You know, you need something hot and spicy to munch along with a drink.'

Dr Kapoor, a friend of Sahir and also his doctor, would join the Scotch session. A well-known heart surgeon, Dr Kapoor, like Sahir, was a heart patient. Sahir would often pull his leg—'Doctor, should I come to see you (to enquire after your health) or to show myself to you (as a patient)?'

This is exactly what happened that fateful night.

In the intervening years, Sahir had built his own house—Parchhaiyan, while Dr Kapoor lived in a bungalow at Versova, a sea-swept Mumbai village. Jadu had attained fame as a writer.

One evening Sahir went to Dr Kapoor's. Heart surgeon Dr Thakur was supposed to be there. I think producer-director Ramanand Sagar was there too—or did he come in a little later?

They started a game of cards to cheer up Dr Kapoor. While distributing cards, Dr Kapoor realised that something was terribly wrong with Sahir—his face was pale, muscles contorted and he was trying to muffle pain. Dr Kapoor almost screamed, 'Sahir...'

Sahir collapsed.

Attempts were made to resuscitate him, but he was dead. Amidst unprecedented chaos, Dr Kapoor was sent away to Sagar's house—at the behest of the film-maker. Anwar, Sahir's driver, was terribly shaken; he was asked to guard the dead body.

Yash Chopra, a close friend of Sahir, was away in Srinagar. Javed arrived in a cab; his chauffeur had taken the day off. He took Sahir to Parchhaiyan by the same cab. Anwar and the cabbie both carried the body up to Sahir's first-floor flat.

When he first saw Sahir lying lifeless at Dr Kapoor's residence, Javed was speechless. However, on reaching Parchhaiyan he broke down, hugged Sahir and wept. 'I didn't cry like this in my entire life.'

It was one in the morning. No one knew what to do, whom to call. Javed sat next to Sahir. Alone. Dazed and devastated. Soon, neighbours arrived. A kind soul said, 'Tie the two arms together; the body is getting stiff.' Javed was carrying out all orders—mechanically, even as he was weeping.

In the morning someone called up Sahir's friends and colleagues. People made a beeline for Parchhaiyan to pay their last respects to the great poet. Dhurries were spread, chairs were set aside to make space for mourners.

When Javed came down to supervise the funeral arrangements he saw the cabbie. 'Arre, you are still here? Why did you not tell me? How much is your fare?' The cabbie was a civilised man. He joined hands and said, 'I didn't hang around here for money, sahab. Where could I go at midnight?'

Javed dipped into his wallet. 'No sahab...let it be...sahab,' the driver pleaded repeatedly.

Javed yelled at him, 'Keep this hundred rupee note. Although dead, he has extracted his money from me.' Saying this, Javed broke down once again.

This happened just before Sahir's funeral.

Kuldip Nayar and the Pirsahab

This gem of a story comes from my dear friend, renowned journalist Kuldip Nayar. It goes beyond the pale of logic. Figment of imagination? Hallucination? Spooky? Read on.

Nayar Sahab has for long been a dispassionate chronicler of events that shaped modern India. Held in high esteem for his professional integrity and lucid style, Nayar Sahab is above fear and favour.

Also, Nayar Sahab has been a fierce advocate of the India-Pakistan friendship. He firmly believes that people-to-people contact will go a long way to forge peace and harmony in the subcontinent.

Every year he and his friends—writers, artists and thinkers—visit the Wagah border on the eve of Independence Day. They light candles under a star-lit sky, and raise slogans to commemorate the India-Pakistan friendship.

In 1998, I joined Nayar Sahab's cavalcade.

The road to Wagah is straight like an arrow. The drive was smooth and the air, sweet. We got talking.

Nayar Sahab said, 'Suppose I take this road and saunter into Pakistan; no checkposts, no visa, no frisking. Will I be going there to plunder that country? Aren't there enough plunderers on both sides of the divide? Do they need an outsider?'

Nayar Sahab has a deep bond with Sialkot, his birthplace, which is now in Pakistan. 'I remember my school, my teachers—Dinanath Master and Maulavi Ismail. My slate-pencil, book of alphabets...everything is lying there. My roots are in the soil of Sialkot; few branches were torn off and planted here,' he said with a sigh.

He recalled his house in Sialkot—a sprawling structure with

a spacious courtyard. No walls, no boundaries; a large peepal (fig) tree—and a tomb. No one knew how it came there. According to Nayar Sahab's mother, it was the tomb of an unknown 'pir', and was thus known as pir ki qabar.

The matriarch's world revolved round the peepal and the tomb. The two sentinels cemented her faith in life. Every morning, she would sprinkle a bit of vermillion on the tree and wipe off her finger on the tomb. A lamp lit as a mark of respect to the fig tree was placed near the tomb. The crimson, warm flame linked the two.

A tree, a tomb and a lamp. I found the image fascinating; it symbolised India's pluralistic culture—the 'Ganga-Jamuni tehzeeb'.

Nayar Sahab's mother would consult the pirsahab on family matters. 'She would often sit by the tomb and talk with the pirsahab. To the rest of the world, he was dead and gone, a relic of Sialkot's hazy past. However, my mother believed that he was alive and was a part of Nayar Sahab's family—a trusted friend, a wise counsellor,' he said.

On the day of exams, children would leave home only after bowing before the tomb. 'My mother would often 'see' the pirsahab in her dream,' said Nayar Sahab, even as blurred images of childhood flickered before his eyes.

We reached Wagah.

The sun was setting. Flags were being brought down amidst the paying of obeisance by the blowing of trumpets and beating of drums. A group of Pakistan nationals was present too. At midnight we lit candles and raised slogans celebrating the India-Pakistan friendship. Some were moved to tears, others were calm. The next day we reached Amritsar airport to take the New Delhi flight.

Meanwhile, the pirsahab had begun to grow on me; I wanted to know more about him—how did he look? Did Nayar Sahab's mother ever talk about 'seeing' him, the way he dressed, his demeanour?

I was taken aback when Nayar Sahab said that he too had 'seen' the holy man. 'The pirsahab looked exactly as my mother had described him,' he said and recounted a story.

It so happened that on 25 June 1975, Indira Gandhi declared Emergency amidst political instability, labour and student unrest and inflation. The press was gagged; civil liberties were curtailed, and Opposition stalwarts and journalists were packed off to jail.

That fateful Friday morning Nayar Sahab walked into the dreaded Tihar prison as the government's 'honoured guest'.

The jail superintendent tried to pacify Nayar Sahab by saying that he would be set free soon. Hope was Nayar Sahab's only faithful ally.

Who had given the arrest orders?

'Madam', the official said in a conspiratorial tone.

Days wore on and chances of an early release seemed bleak. Resigned to fate, Nayar Sahab decided to go back to writing and reading. He asked the jail supremo for books and a writing pad; the latter gave him a table and a table lamp as well. Tender mercies!

A distraught Nayar Sahab prayed for the good, old pirsahab's intervention. 'And he did appear in my dream. Long beard—he was dressed in a green cloak. Exactly as my mother had seen him. I can't recollect if he was wearing a headgear,' he said.

The pirsahab assured the Sialkot lad that he would be set free the following Thursday. He also asked for a shawl as it was terribly cold in the damp, old Sialkot tomb.

Nayar Sahab was a free bird on Friday, 11 September 1975. The jail superintendent told him that the release order was actually signed and sealed on Thursday (exactly as the pirsahab had predicted); it's just that the junior official reported late for work, and the jail superintendent was busy with files. Hence, the order fell into Nayar Sahab's hand on Friday. A tad apprehensive, the superintendent wondered if Nayar Sahab had prior intimation about his release order.

'Yes, I knew about it,' Nayar Sahab replied with a smile.

Nayar Sahab's mother insisted that he should go to Sialkot and place a chaadar on the tomb. However, his travel plan fell through as Pakistan's visa rules were draconian. Meanwhile, his mother died in 1980, and Nayar Sahab had an irresistible urge to visit Sialkot.

Sialkot had undergone a drastic change; a family was camping in Nayar Sahab's house. Small shops had sprouted around the courtyard. Neither could he find the pir's tomb nor the fig tree—although he remembered the spot where the tree once stood. Residents knew nothing about the tomb.

During his stay in Sialkot, Nayar Sahab made inquiries about the missing tomb. A shopkeeper who he used to meet every day turned out to be a good ally. The day Nayar Sahab was to leave for India, the shopkeeper caught sight of him in the market and came to him. 'Sir, there indeed was a tomb right next to our shop. But we moved it out for lack of space.'

On his return, Nayar Sahab placed a chaadar on the tomb of Nizamuddin Auliya, the legendary Sufi saint.

The good, old 'pir' never re-appeared in Nayar Sahab's dream. 'With my mother dead, he too was gone. Both attained "mukti" (liberation), I suppose,' he said with a grin.

Raavi Paar

Circumstances grabbed Darshan Singh by the throat. Actually, the sheer gravity and inevitability of incidents should have turned him insane; surprisingly enough, Darshan Singh didn't go mad.

It all began with his father's death. His mother then immersed herself in gurdwara services. And his wife gave birth to twins.

Darshan Singh didn't know whether to celebrate or mourn. It was providence playing its pet 'give-with-one-hand-and-take-away-with-another' trick, and Darshan was helpless.

Word went round that Independence was on its way. Who knew when it would reach Lyalpur. Hindus and Sikhs would meet clandestinely in the gurdwara. Shahani was moaning in pain, her first pregnancy.

Every day Darshan Singh would bring home sad stories—of massacre, mayhem and migration.

Father would pacify him, 'Nothing wrong will happen, beta. Has a single house, whether of a Hindu or a Sikh, been attacked so far?'

'Bhapa-ji, the gurdwara has been attacked, no? Attempts were made twice to set it aflame.'

'True, but you all seek shelter under the roof of the gurdwara, isn't it?'

Darshan Singh would keep silent. Bhapa-ji was right. But every soul had left home and sought refuge there.

This happened a fortnight ago.

Late in the night, there was a loud thud, as if something had come crashing down. Everyone huddled in the courtyard. Cries of *'Jo boley so nihal'* came from the gurdwara. Bhapa-ji rushed to the terrace. As he was coming down the staircase he slipped and fell on a spade in the courtyard; the blade pierced his head. He died.

Darshan Singh performed Bhapa-ji's final rites, hurriedly stuffed the family's precious jewellery into pillow covers, and fled to the gurdwara with everyone. People were struck with fear, but felt secure in each other's company. So did Darshan Singh, his mother and wife. Darshan was calm. He said, 'We aren't alone. If no one else, at least our Waheguru is with us.'

A band of volunteers supervised the arrangements. People had brought with them wheat flour, pulses and ghee. The langar was working 24×7. But how long would it last? People were hopeful that the government would send some help.

Someone asked, 'Which government are we talking about? The Britishers have just left.'

'Pakistan has been created, but they are yet to form a government.'

'Some people say the army is in charge and they escort refugees to safety—the Line of Control.'

'Refugees? What does that mean?'

'Refugees are refugees.'

'Never heard this word before.'

A group of families could take it no more. They left the gurdwara.

People would meet and talk. Many were desperate as the future seemed bleak. 'They said trains have started. We should go to the station. How long are we going to sit here?'

'True, we'll have step out—I know it's risky, but...Waheguru is not going to carry us on his shoulders.' Someone quoted from the *Gurbani*: 'Nanak is the name of a ship; those who board it are led safely to the other shore.'

When people left the gurdwara, it was as if a bubble had bobbed up from the void. It would eventually pop as new entrants brought more news from the world outside.

'The railway station looks like a camp.'

'People are dying of starvation and overeating as well. They are wrecked by all kinds of ailments.'

It was Makar Sankranti the next day. There was Akhand Paath in the gurdwara, the non-stop reading of the Holy Book. On such an auspicious day Shahani gave birth to two boys—one was rickety and weak with hardly any chance of survival. That night someone brought the news:

'A special train has come to take refugees across the border. Come along, get ready.' A big crowd was set to leave the gurdwara. Darshan Singh joined them; so did Shahani, although she looked pale and weak.

However, mother flatly refused. 'I'll come later, beta. Take your wife and kids along and get going...Be safe,' she told her son.

Darshan insisted, tried hard to persuade his mother. Eventually, the granthi (religious preacher) said, 'You all go. We shall leave one by one—and cross the LOC. Bijee (mother) will come with us.'

Darshan Singh joined the group. He kept the newborn twins in a bamboo basket with a proper cover. It looked like a vegetable hamper.

The train was waiting at the station. It was packed like a can of sardines. Many who sat on the roof looked like blades of grass sprouting from the mud. Moved by the plight of a frail woman, cradling newborn twins and trying to get into the train, some made space for her on the roof.

After nearly ten hours, the refugee train showed some sign of life—it moved, making a loud, creaky sound. Evening appeared on the horizon, her face smeared with blood.

With two babies suckling hungrily, Shahani's breasts looked sagged and dry. She would keep aside one baby and hold the other one to her chest. Wrapped in a dirty dupatta, the babies looked as if picked from a wayside dustbin.

At night Darshan Singh realised that one of the kids was active; cooing and crying, while the other lay still like a log of wood. Darshan shoved his hand into the basket to check. The boy had turned lifeless—cold.

Others came to know as Darshan began to sob. They wanted to take away the dead baby from Shahani. However, she sat motionless, holding the basket close to her chest, in a daze.

'They are twins...One brother wouldn't drink milk without the other,' she said in whispering tone. Shahani wouldn't loosen her grip on the basket.

The train stopped, started and stopped again. Darkness reigned everywhere. People kept guessing about the next station.

'Hmmm. Khairabad is gone.'

'This is Gujranwala, certainly.'

'Just an hour's journey. When Lahore comes, we will cross over to India.'

Happy that the destination was within reach, people began to raise slogans.

'Har Har Mahadeo.'

'*Jo boley so nihal.*'

The train was crossing a bridge. Everyone was elated, crazy with joy.

'Here's Raavi.'

'Which means Lahore has come.'

Amidst chaos someone whispered to Darshan Singh, 'Sardar-ji, throw the boy's dead body into the Raavi. May God bless him. Why lug it across the river?'

Darshan Singh tried to pull the basket from his wife. Then, all of a sudden, he lifted the baby boy wrapped in the dupatta and tossed him into the womb of the Raavi, shouting, Waheguru.

A child's soft cry pierced the heart of darkness.

A bewildered Darshan looked at Shahani. She was holding the dead child in her frail arms.

A collective roar rent the air:
'Wagah, Wagah...'
'Hindustan Zindabad...'

Flashback

Bimal Roy was my guru. I learnt a lot from him. I most certainly owe him a big debt. I have, through my writing, drawn a portrait of Bimal-da.

The placid face of a river flows quietly into the evening mist
Lamps of eyes burn amidst the wheat-complexioned mist
The cigarette smoke smouldering incessantly
The faraway dim voice drowned in slumber;
Beneath the flying shadows of unknown dreams
Contours of a face melt like wax
Transforms after listening to the melody of new dreams,
Looks like he will neither sleep, nor will he wake up—nor speak
The placid face of a river flows in the evening mist

I have also written a biographical short story on Bimal-da. About that some other day.

Amrit Kumbh was my first film script for Bimal-da. Well-known Bengali writer Samaresh Basu's novel on a stampede during the mammoth Kumbh congregation, raises several metaphysical questions about people and faith. Thousands perished in the 1954 tragedy.

Bimal-da was all set to make a film on Samaresh Basu's searing novel. We took almost three years to complete the script during which time Bimal-da made *Bandini* and *Kabuliwala.*

As we were getting ready for the outdoor shoot of *Amrit Kumbh*, Bimal-da fell ill. He asked us to go to Allahabad and shoot the pilgrimage sequences. Kamal-da asked him, 'Bimal-da, why do you insist on making this film?' Kamal-da was our cameramen.

Bimal-da replied, 'The novelist has created the character of a man in quest of nectar (amrit). I think I am the man.

I too am searching for amrit.'

Bimal-da passed away on 8 January 1965. That very day the kumbh mela got off to a start in Allahabad. The film was never made; but the script is safe in my archives.

How do I make a film?

Well, I don't have a surefire formula, and I think there is none. Everything begins to fall in line once I choose a story. It may not be written by me. I select from among the many I have read.

Cinema is a genre with its own autonomy and aesthetics; it follows its trajectory even if inspired by a literary work. Writers often accuse film-makers of tampering with their novels or short stories. However, these are professional hazards.

A script is the film's spine; its raison d'etre. It entails lot of paperwork—fleshing out characters, delineating their growth and mannerisms, how would they converse with each other, how would they look on the screen and so forth. I never go on the set without a full-fledged script.

When the film is canned, it goes on the editing table, where it gets its final shape and form. 'The End' marks a new beginning for the film-maker.

Film-making is a nuts-and-bolts job; one learns a lot on the set.

What inspires me to make a film?

Like all artists and writers, I like probing human relationships, and a whole lot of emotions—good, bad and ugly—that go to make or unmake them.

I delve deep into human experiences. Imbued in myriad hues and musical notes, relationships nourish my poems and films.

I hold life's finger and try to reach the ultimate truth. I may not succeed a hundred per cent—however, the effort matters. Cinema may be a world of make-believe, but it tackles the bald truths of human life. Picasso has said that all art is false, but it takes you to the eternal truth. Emotions are as real as a festering wound and a film-maker unravels them with the help of the camera and lights, characters and script.

What do I think of my audience?

I am open to criticism. I want to know how viewers have received my film. I don't belittle them. Eventually, it is up to them and they give their verdict without fear or favour. Not all can grasp every nuance, each frame. Viewers have their likes and dislikes, wisdom and perception, which a film-maker must respect. Period.

Sound in my films?

Art disdains clamour and chaos. It speaks amidst silence. Art has a tenuous link with contemplation and mindfulness and I never lose sight of this thought when I am writing or making a film. I promise myself—I want to make a good film, I am going to put my heart and mind into it; I owe it to viewers. That's all.

My characters?

I invest my characters with identity. Moreover, the camera too speaks and adds inputs to the film. Ditto with lights, music and editing. I would say a film is like the Berlin Philharmonic orchestra.

In *Koshish*, Sanjeev Kumar and Jaya Bhaduri communicate effortlessly despite the fact that neither can hear or speak. This happens because other characters are in conversation with each other, thus adding eloquence to the couple's silence.

Poetry and humour help me shape characters. You will find my characters laughing—but I refrain from vulgarity. I don't like humour being used to belittle others. Being a pucca Mumbaikar I have realised that the labour class laugh a lot.

A loader or an engine driver often comes up with an evocative line which may be better than a poem. I keep my ears close to the ground.

I am a workaholic. Work keeps me going. Equally powerful is the pull of love—pure, unceasing love. Love reigns supreme in India's ancient 'rasa' theory. Love not just for friends and those dear to me but for the mankind. Human civilisations have celebrated universal love.

Flashbacks?

I must share with you my trade secret. I love flashbacks. Of all the films I have made, *Achanak* (1973) has most flashbacks. It's my favourite cinematic device which gives the film a languid back-and-forth rhythm, and deepens its content.

Memories maketh a person. When two friends meet up in

a cafe on a bright Sunday afternoon, they go back in time and exchange memories, songs, jokes and stories—the stuff films are made of.

Film-makers are like carpenters. When a carpenter makes a chair, he conjures up an image in his mind and follows it till the final product is ready—well-oiled, well-polished. A film-maker's task is to transfer to the silver screen a clutch of images which, when strung together, tell a story.

Your favourite haunt?

My mind buzzes like a beehive when I sit down to write the script. I wrote most scripts in a Bangalore (now Bengaluru) hotel. From the airport I and my AD would drive straight to Hotel West End. A quick breakfast and we would begin work, and go on till late night. No sightseeing, no parties.

Nestled amidst tall trees, the hotel looked like a hermit's abode. I take ten to twelve days—say a fortnight, to complete the first draft of the script. The next day I am back in Mumbai.

The song situations are marked too. *'Mera kuchhh samaan tumhare paas padha hai'*, the *Ijaazat* song, hit my mind when I was writing the film's script. Songs can't be pasted on films. Both are inseparable.

Meena Kumari

I read Meena-ji's will which stated clearly that she had given me all her poems and the rights thereof. Actually, a poet's right is confined only to the process of creation. The moment a poem comes to life, it is handed over to readers and connoisseurs. My right is to safeguard the rights of her legatees.

I could never hold the hand, nor the 'daaman'
Someone got up and passed me by closely

Meena-ji passed away. She would often say:

It would be a long wait—for centuries
I shall take leave of this lonely world

She left the world to its fate—to suffer loneliness. She took away with her an entire era. All her life she prayed, said Amen, got up and left. As long as she lived, she gathered pain and internalised it. She said:

The day finished in pieces
Night came in fragments

Your share matches the size
Of your 'aanchal';

When I thought of understanding the urges of the heart
I heard the sound of laughs
As if someone was saying
Yet another defeat,

No conversation, no dialogue
Keep walking the whole day
Even when I met someone dear
It brought restlessness along

Meena-ji's heart was deep as the ocean. It spilled over and ended. Her death made pain an orphan; there has been no one to caress grief. Once I did a pen sketch of hers in the form of a poem:

Sitting on a mulberry tree someone
Spins threads of silk
Opening moments upon moments
Weaving every leaf,
Hears the cadence of every breath, this mad woman
Opens every breath and wraps it around her body

Caught in the web of the threads
This poet of silken sensibilities will one day
Be smothered by its own threads—and die

On reading the poem she laughed, and said, 'You know, of course, what these threads mean—love. I am in love with love; in love with the feeling, the realisation of love; in love with love's name. If one dies wrapping so much love around one's body, then what more should one want?'

I have before me one of her pages. It reads:

I thought of love, I looked for love
Discovered cool desires
The mud of the soul, such sweet smell
On hot, prickly, naked roads
Running barefoot, stopped

Earned a little warmth from the sun for the wounds of shadow
And saw in the shadow sores inflicted by the sun
Within me was love suffused with fragrance
But oh! I was looking outside.

The journey from the external world to the inner space was a long one for which Meena-ji spent her entire life. There were forests, deserts and mountains along the way. That's why she said:

The sores on the feet happened while trudging through a forest
Or else who would light a lamp in the storm?
In every small particle were engraved virgin bows
Every statue was made by self,
And if came across a philosopher's stone
Must have remembered heart.

Meena-ji loved the sores on her feet. She became used to walking on thorns:

Might have quenched the thirst of burning thorns
Might have celebrated the oozing water in the hollow of hands

Meena-ji's life was big, not long. Life came to her in moments and minutes and she lived by moments and minutes. She never fled from a sad moment nor did she try to humour herself to escape such moments. In fact, she embraced each moment of anguish—and wept, and emerged with greater strength and lustre—like a flower which looks resplendent because of dewdrops.

And when she laughed heartily, it seemed as if a new day had been born—yet another moment, one more day. Sometimes a night, a week or a month, but she never got a chunk of years to live. Had she been blessed with a long life, she would have grown weary. For her every day was a beginning. She says:

The beginning happens
But not the end
When in my story
That name is absent
When a traveller gets lost
In the darkness of tresses
He gets a bad name—
But not anonymity;
Why shouldn't I collect, with a smile on my lips,
Fragments of a broken heart?
There is no reward written
In the fate of every person

There were a few images which flickered before her eyes. A white desert, a gulmohar bent on the bank of a river or a boat sinking in a mist-filled river. If she saw the face of a dream, she would transcreate it into a couplet:

The day has sunk into the water
Or a boat with a marriage party has gone down
But there is no commotion
On the bank

Hidden in that single personality were countless faces. She wore the faces of the characters she portrayed on the screen. Never pulled them down. Films were done and finished, but the characters lived on with her. Some such faces stayed with her till the last—'Bibi', 'Sahibjan', 'Didi', 'Mahjabeen'... It often happened that Meena would tell her face:

It's only once in a while that I'll get to see you
Wear your veil, I'll unveil you,

See drops of sweat on the moon's brow
Whenever I'll call you 'Mahjabeen'.

It was a simple Urdu couplet; but she insisted on changing the line. 'No, I don't want my name (Mahjabeen) in the couplet.' I changed the line, but today I think the line with her name in it was so true. The revised lines read as follows:

See drops of sweat
On the moon's brow
When I'll call you
By your name

I'll beat my forehead again and again;
If my prayers were inadequate
If there is no reply from my destination
I'll keep looking back and calling you
When the flame of night
Begins to flicker at dawn
I'll get up and untangle your hair.

But when the starlit night's flame did flicker, the hand which was to untangle hair, couldn't reach the moon:

How lonely is the moon and the sky
My heart which has met me at many places is lonely too
All hopes are lost, stars have gone into hiding
A line of smoke quivers, alone
Is this called life?
Where body is lonely, soul too
Even if one meets a fellow traveller
Both keep walking, alone

It would be a long wait—for centuries
I shall take leave of this lonely world

I wrote a tribute to the story of a 'Tragedian' as she was always referred in the media.

Girado Parda Ke Daastan Khaali Ho Gai Hai.

Bring down the curtain
The story is over
Bring down the curtain
A beautiful, sad face
Is lost somewhere in space,
Miffed with impoverished eyes
Tears begin to roll down
Voices have parted ways with musical notes

Silence of deep feelings, awareness
Echoes in the air,
All-pervading darkness of completeness
Burns

Meena Didi

Three miracles happened in a row. She came here, stayed here and...

The day had just begun—like a light, happy drizzle. She kept the little girl in a small garden in the studio and left. As simple as 'You play here, OK? I'll be back soon.'

She then got down to give a bath to Rajjo, her dear duck, in a nearby pond. While the reluctant duck was trying to run away and get back to swimming, the girl made strident efforts to get a firm grip on her and clean her wings. The duck sprinkled water on the girl's hair. She guffawed heartily. A new-born laugh—pure and sparkling.

A lot of dust had got stuck on the girl's hair. Her clothes were shabby, as if she had returned home from a long journey. The gardener who was sleeping on a mat in the courtyard began to yell at the girl; her laughter had disrupted his sleep.

'Aye, go way from here,' he shrieked.

Unperturbed, she took Rajjo in her arms, and tied a clean piece of cloth on her left leg, removing the old one. She then stepped into the studio canteen with Rajjo in tow, walking with spunk as if she knew everyone present there.

She asked the teawalla, a young boy, for a hot cup. 'Just go away from here,' he screamed, finding her overfamiliar style of talking a bit irksome.

That very moment Rajjo rushed to the tea boy and caught his trousers with her beak; the boy was shell-shocked and, as he ran out, he tripped and hot tea spilled all over his clothes. The girl laughed heartily, embraced Rajjo and lightly patted her on the back.

The boy stood a little away and began to sob. The girl walked up to him and pacified him, saying that she would box

Rajjo's ear. She pulled out from her bag a piece of cloth and cleaned his hands, feet and hair, speaking with him as if she was a wise woman who knew the ways of the world. With all the attention he got from the girl, the teawalla felt better. People around them began to giggle.

The girl went back to the canteen and asked for tea. The man at the counter was caressing coins, his daily booty. He smiled wickedly and said, 'No chai without money. Go and get some money.' The girl couldn't take her eyes off the coins in the box. She replied, 'Why? You've so much money. Why wouldn't you give me tea?'

'Tea isn't free, understand?' he yelled at her.

'But you have so much money,' she said.

The shop owner was both amused and amazed. How strange—a minute ago she seemed mature and wise and now a fragile, little girl, he thought. He smiled, sat her down and asked the boy to give her a hot cuppa. Still reeling from the shock, the boy placed a cup before the girl.

She took two biscuits from the jar, ate one and gave the other to Rajjo. The shop owner was livid. He had a strong urge to throw them out. But he dropped the idea and placed the jar on the next table—out of the girl's reach.

Done with her breakfast, the girl picked up her cloth bag and Rajjo jumped out of the chair, as if on cue. Both sauntered out of the canteen. Those present were taken aback.

Who is this girl? they wondered. Doesn't she realise that this is a cinema studio where crooked people are in abundant supply. And what is this duck doing here? Good lord, they thought. The canteen boy was watching the bizarre pair with curiosity from a distance.

'She should be in a film, yaar—she is yummy,' croaked a bystander, showing his broken tooth.

The girl stretched on the gardener's mat, her eyes heavy with sleep. Lying next to her was Rajjo. Both went off to sleep. After a while Rajjo woke up; the girl was asleep. Rajjo shed a little of her fatigue by fluttering her wings animatedly.

Rajjo tweaked the girl's cheeks with her beak, patted her hair with affection, tickled her foot and began to cluck-cluck in an attempt to stir her from sleep. The girl got up and began to chase her; both jumped into the pond. They sprinkled water on each other playfully. Their laughter had the fragrance of fresh, wholesome milk. The gardener yelled at them.

'What have we stolen from you? We haven't made the water dirty, have we? We are just playing,' the girl said. The gardener was unmoved. He thought he owned the water. He shooed them away. The girl and Rajjo went back to the canteen. They were hungry.

'Give us food,' the girl told the man at the counter. This time around he showed them out. 'Who the hell are you?' he asked.

'I am Meenakshi,' the girl said.

The canteen man was startled.

'Don't you know me? I am Meena didi,' the girl said. Bystanders laughed raucously.

'Oh...she is Meena Kumari? Great,' the man with a broken tooth grinned from ear to ear. They all left, saying, 'Some mad woman, yaar. Forget it.' The girl and Rajjo kept wandering in search of food. As night threw a dark veil over the studio, the girl slept by a wall next to the stage, hungry and tired. At midnight the girl heard the tea boy telling her in soft whispers,

'Take this, eat.' The girl woke up Rajjo, and asked the boy to join them—bread, vegetables and some sprouts.

'I've eaten,' the boy replied.

'What is your name?' the girl asked.

'Me? I am *chhokra*,' he said. Rajjo showed her displeasure by turning her head away.

'OK, I am going to call you Mannu,' the girl said. The boy liked the name. A bright smile lit up his face—a new name and that too with a meaning.

'Have you met Meena Kumari?' the boy asked the girl.

'No,' she replied. 'How does she look?'

'That I can't say, but her voice is similar to yours,' he said.

'Does she come here?'

'Well, she comes if she has a shooting here.'

'Next time she comes tell her I live here...Ask her to meet me,' the girl said.

'OK,' the boy replied, his voice had a tinge of sadness as he knew that there was no way he could fulfil the girl's wish. 'What will you tell her if you happen to meet her?' he asked.

'I'll marry her,' the girl replied.

'What?'

'Haa...haa...haaa, poor fellow,' she laughed.

Everything about this girl is eerie, he thought. However, he made a resolve that he would take her to Meena didi whenever didi visits the studio.

That night the boy slept next to the girl.

The next day Mannu took charge of the meals. He also made a room for them to rest—at the back of the store room amidst dismantled sets. The place was a tad creepy—it had just a half-ceiling; the walls would sway and there were pillars as well—some standing straight, some head over heels. A palanquin meant to ferry a newlywed bride to her husband's home was lying in a corner, belonging neither to the bride's father nor her in-laws. Next to it was a broken throne. It is said that ages ago an empress would sit on it with regal aloofness.

A little away stood the empress, cast in, perhaps, marble, looking sad and lonely—knowing well that she was not going to get back her throne anytime soon. Clocks were frozen in time. The place was freakish and surreal. Time was split into small cubes. Choose between the mummified past or a shiny-sheeny future.

The girl got used to the studio, as if she was living there for ages. People around her were amused. 'Where are your homes, people?' some would ask her.

'Don't know,' she would reply.

'Where have you come from?'

'Faraway place. There are white mountains there.'

'Who lives there?'

'No one.'

'How did you come here?'

'On foot.'

'Alone?'

'No...I and Rajjo.'

People would be left baffled.

One day a man from the production department gave her new clothes: a salwar, kurta and a round cap. She looked like a shepherd's daughter. Rajjo nearly attacked her, bit her and ran away with her cap. The girl chased her down, held her. Such great fun! Both would fight, play and giggle. And re-unite.

Once Rajjo stole the girl's cap and quietly sneaked it into her little cradle. On finishing her bath, the girl realised that the cap was missing. She asked Rajjo—first with patience and then with exasperation. She even yelled at her. Later, she found the cap in her basket. The girl was annoyed. Mannu pacified his didi.

Mannu's didi was liked by all—especially the little ones. She would play with them, leap into the pond, offer a piece of advice to seniors or reprimand someone. She would have a whale of time with children—she would be the youngest robber in the thief-police game or dress as a priestess. Also, she would gather dry, withered flowers from the garden, without the gardener's knowledge, and arrange them artistically in one of the studio rooms.

Mannu wanted didi only to himself. He wanted to take her to those who didn't know her—and tell them with pride, 'Look, didi is mine.'

But who is she, dear?

Can't say—wife, sister, mother. All rolled into one. Mannu felt sad and dejected. He seemed like an illiterate person who is gifted a fat book to read. Tears began to roll down his cheeks. 'But she is mine, only mine,' he screamed. Mute thoughts exploded terribly, leaving him shattered.

Didi, who was sitting nearby, was taken aback. 'What happened, Mannu?' she asked.

'Nothing,' he said, stifling a sob.

'Why are you crying?' asked didi and held him close. Rajjo too began to cluck in a soft voice to pacify him—pure, wordless affection.

One evening Rajjo began to laugh uncontrollably. She guffawed so much that she had severe stomach pain. Didi and Mannu too joined the laughter club. However, didi was scared when Rajjo began to writhe in pain, her muscles contorting.

Didi soon realised that Rajjo was tipsy. 'What have you done, Rajjo,' she exclaimed. Rajjo took didi to a nearby spot and showed her the bottle of liquor. Rajjo was giggling and dancing. There was some stuff left in the bottle. Both Mannu and didi emptied it and laughed till they turned insane.

Mannu slept on the cracked throne, didi, in her tent, while Rajjo swayed in her little cradle. Rajjo sang for a while and then stopped. Mannu and didi were fast asleep, not Rajjo. She was wide awake.

One can't quantify time in the cloistered world of a film studio. There is hardly any difference between hours and centuries. Didi defied Time. She was innocent as ever. Untamed, fearless. Rajjo, of course, changed a lot. Vulnerable and sensitive to a fault. She would get upset over small things. Actually, Rajjo would have left didi and retired to a forest. Or turn a 'sanyasini'. Poor creature. She couldn't think of leaving didi.

There was a piece of land behind the studio where a band of wandering nomads had pitched their tents. Rajjo would sit on the rear wall and watch them for hours, thinking that if they left for their next destination, she would join them. How nice it would be, she thought. While passing through a deep forest she would find a lake where she would swim for God knows how many days or months—and then sleep there forever. A drop in the water.

'Raaje,' didi called aloud. Rajjo looked at her. 'Oh God, how can I leave this poor, little girl who knows nothing about life. I'll leave her after she gets married,' Rajjo told herself. Didi changed the piece of cloth tied around Rajjo's bruised leg.

Rajjo's beak touched didi's chin. Rajjo was looking at her

intently, as if saying, 'Child, you are my mother, aren't you?'

The studio store room had undergone a change. Some pillars had turned to ash. The old throne's back was broken. The ceiling had developed too many cracks. New doors, opening on both sides, had arrived. There was a moon lying in a corner, torn to pieces. But, didi hadn't changed a bit. She was on an endless journey.

Mannu cast a glance everywhere. The morning looked as fresh as the season's first shower. Ditto was the morning which had brought didi to the studio.

Mannu went to didi's palanquin. 'Didi,' he called her aloud, rubbing his eyes. Didi was arranging a hundred little things in the palanquin. 'This is my treasure trove,' she said with pride.

'Oh, good! Where did you get these from? Did you buy them, didi?' Mannu asked her.

'No, I did everything on my own,' didi replied. She had gathered a whole lot of quaint, little things: a pair of wooden sandals and a shell; a small box with fragments of bangles; a matchbox with a peacock's sketch embossed on it; a few red and yellow stones; a cap with a pompom, a few clothes and toys.

'What will you do with this?' Mannu asked.

'Mannu, this has to be guarded zealously. You get a good husband if you have a big treasure trove,' she said.

'Says who?' he asked.

'Well, I don't know, but it is said.'

Mannu was confused but happy that didi had no answer to his question.

Didi began to look for Rajjo; she wasn't in the cradle. 'Where is Rajjo?' didi asked Mannu. He didn't know either. She must have gone for a swim, didi said to herself and walked to the pond. Mannu went to the canteen.

And then something unusual happened. While Mannu had just reached the canteen, he saw Meena Kumari's swanky, ship-like car entering the studio gate. His heart began to pound and blood began to run faster through his veins.

'Meena didi.'

'Rajjo...'

'Cluck-cluck.'

Two-three voices blended together. Three-four lives fused into each other and a shriek pierced the sky. A lifeless bubble soared high and fell down the very next second. A glass broke into small pieces. Mannu was holding didi's kurta. There was no one in the car. It whizzed past didi and Mannu and sped away, honking brazenly.

Rajjo, smeared with blood, was in didi's arms. 'Meena-didi...' Mannu called aloud. She ran out of the studio, screaming 'Rajjo...Rajjo', Mannu followed her—and the third miracle happened.

Some say that no one saw the girl leaving the studio. Still others say that they saw a sanyasin instead, her hair as white as snow.

My Right Hands

Farhana Mahmood

Do you know how a tree comes to life? The sun grabs it by the hair and pulls it up from the soil. The tree slowly begins to breathe and tries to get on its feet. Water, soil, sunlight, air and manure do their job. The tree re-affirms its roots and soon begins to sway sensuously to a breezy rhythm.

Farhana Mahmood

I have gathered my sunlight, air, water and manure from many gurus and colleagues.

There is nothing self-made about humans. People, big and small, help us grow—knowingly or otherwise—and come to terms with life.

I am talking of the hands that have grown from my arms, and fingers that have sprouted from my hands.

Those were the years, around 2000–2001, when I was working on *Tehreer Munshi Premchand Ki*, a television serial for Doordarshan Kendra. It was based on *Godan* and *Nirmala*, Premchand-ji's novels, and a number of his acclaimed short stories. The script work was huge.

Since I write in Urdu, I was looking for someone who could type out the manuscript in Urdu on the computer. I called up Urdu Markaz, a well-known computer centre in central

Mumbai, and asked them to recommend a suitable candidate. One fine morning Farhana was at my office. Believe me, I got one more right hand.

Farhana belongs to a family which is familiar with Urdu language. Her father had participated in the trade union movement helmed by the Communist Party of India. Farhana too has leftist leanings. I admire her for her qualities: she is straightforward and disciplined in her work.

Her two sisters, who are heavily into needlework and crochet, learned designing on the computer at the Urdu Markaz. So did Farhana, but she transcended her boundaries.

Quiet and self-assured, Farhana reminds me of Cinderella's fairy godmother. She wears many hats: handles my Urdu correspondence on the e-mail; guards my manuscripts and books; pulls out printouts (she is amazingly tech-savvy) with the alacrity of a magician; and digs out references for me in a jiffy. Moreover, she comes to my rescue when I can't for the life of me recall a couplet or a poem.

My fifty books have so far been published under her vigil. Farhana has a flair for language. She once told me, 'I started working for you in 2003, and am still going strong in the twenty-first century!'

A collection of my poems, compiled by her, has been published in Pakistan. I have dedicated some of my books to her. Every time I write a foreword to my book, her name appears invariably in the copy.

My aides and colleagues in office and at home often seek her advice on social, financial and digital matters. I think she will soon turn into a trade union leader like her father!

Lal Bawta Zindabad!

Ajay Jain

A tall, young man is pleading with my security guard to let him in. He proclaims with the zeal of a newly convert: 'I want to meet Gulzar-ji, come what may.'

I called him in.

'I want to work with you, Sir,' he said.

'What work would you do?'

'Whatever...but, I want to be with you.'

Ajay Jain

As I said earlier, I was commissioned by the Doordarshan Kendra to do a serial based on *Godan* and *Nirmala*, Munshi Premchand's widely acclaimed novels, and several short stories. It was sixteen hours of work in all. A writer-friend Salim Arif had teamed up with me.

We were looking for a village reminiscent of the 1930s: rugged terrain, simple people, no television antennae. Eventually, we spotted one on the Maharashtra-Gujarat border—it looked straight out of a Premchand novel: drought, poverty, bad roads.

I was thus busy with my television serial and here this man, a callow youth and gate-crasher, tells me that he wants to work with me.

'Anything you ask me to do,' he said, adding, 'I made several attempts to meet you.'

Actually, I am not a recluse. I love meeting people, barring those who come for a selfie!

Ajay Jain apparently belonged to a decent family—lived in the upscale Daryaganj area in New Delhi. He got my Mumbai address from the Mehras, his neighbours who own Rupa Publications, one of India's leading publishing houses. I don't know how Ajay got a whiff of my Premchand serial.

I offered him tea—he politely declined, reiterating firmly that he was ready to work with me. He seemed cool, and I found him tenacious enough to adapt himself to changing circumstances; willing to face the world and, most importantly, eager to work hard.

I liked his home-spun simplicity. I asked him to join me. Our first meeting ended on an affectionate note. Ajay fished out a silver coin from his wallet and placed it respectfully before me, saying, 'Sir, this is my guru dakshina. Before I left Delhi for Mumbai I had gone to my "kul-guru" to seek blessings.'

Since then, the silver coin has been with me—cocooned in my wallet.

Over the years I came to know of his qualities: he has done his CA from London University; has impeccable organising skills, hosts events, including musical soirees. He took me to US twice for poetry reading tours.

Ajay is very dear to me. At times he accompanies me on my journey. If I have to go to, say, Kolkata, he takes a flight to Mumbai, chaperons me to Kolkata, takes good care of me, brings me back home and rushes to the airport to catch the Delhi flight. Such warmth, such commitment.

Alas! Couldn't turn him into a film-maker, which was his wish—and I am sorry about it.

Mujhe ik chhota-sa sikka diya tha chandi ka tumne
Mujhe 'guru dakshina' di thi,
Kaha tha, 'Shishya hoon ab aap ka main'
Mere sar pe guru hone ka zimma rakh diya tha

Main qayal hoon tumhari nek-niyat ka
Tumhari farmabardari pe fakhra hai,
Magar afsos hai tum ko koiee manzil na de paaya
Guru dakshina ka qarz baaqi hai abhi mujh par.

Ramu

Let's talk about Ramu. His ten fingers rustle up mouth-watering dishes for me every day. To tell you the truth, Ramu 'happened' in my life. He reminds me of the time-tested adage that nothing can be planned in life. Not even an omelette!

Ramu

Ramu appeared on my threshold out of the blue and disappeared, and came back again. He keeps going and coming back. Nothing is certain about Ramu—he is like Mirza Ghalib's pension, which was neither here nor there.

A little about Ramu. He belongs to Bihar—Sitamarhi, to be precise. He was a young boy with an adolescent stubble when he began to work for me as a cook.

Soon, he began to shave. One fine morning he shaved—and disappeared.

He returned after his second child, a daughter, was born. Whenever he returns from Sitamarhi he looks weak and feeble, but quickly regains weight in Mumbai. Govind, my son-in-law, once pointed this out to me.

Ramu's stock reply is that he has to take care of his fields back home. He would work with his father, but their ties were considerably strained. When he became exasperated with him, Ramu would return to Mumbai.

Ramu is a sensational cook. He rules over the kitchen with an iron hand, throwing out anyone who tries to encroach on his territory. He speaks migrants' lingo—sharp and clipped. Words roasted in life's furnace.

Ramu often comes up with a trick or two. One day he began to behave abnormally—his whole body was shaking violently and he was muttering something, as if he was seized by some unholy power or spirit—some mumbo-jumbo.

I told Sundar, my driver, and others to take him to the hospital or bring home a sorcerer. In a couple of minutes Ramu was normal. I suspect it was an alibi to go to Sitamarhi.

Once Ramu performed the vanishing trick. I put a call to him on his mobile. He took the call but didn't answer; I could hear the chugging and chuffing of a running train. He probably must have been in a fix—what if I asked him to come back to Mumbai? He had no answer.

He returned after a year.

I took him to task. 'Is this a joke or what? You coming and going as you please? Do you think this is your father's house?'

'That's why I come back here, no?' he replied softly.

Kaiee mulkon ke dastarkhwaan par baitha
Bahut-see daawatein khaayeen safar mein
Zabaan ne zayqe chakkhe jahaan bhar ke

Anaaj sab ke wohi hain, par
Alag culture hain sab ke
Peesne ke aur pakaane ke

Watan wapis pahunchkar, haath dhokar, khaane pe baitha
Wohi Ramu ki phooli roti, aur tadka lagi arahar ki daal

Dakaar aaya;
Alag hi zayqa hota hai culture ka zabaan par
Joh apney hi tawe par pak ke aata hai

Sundar

Sundar is my right hand. He helms the household team. He is my driver, my trusted lieutenant. He is from Kerala—Thiruvananthapuram—one of five brothers. All five of them are experts at the wheel. One used to work for Shah Rukh Khan's production house.

Sundar was a young boy when he attended my wedding—from Rakhee-ji's side. He used to work for her. This was in 1973. When Rakhee-ji sacked him, he came to me. I asked him to join my staff. He used to hold Meghna, my two-year-old daughter's finger, and take her to school. Now it's Samay, my grandson. How time flies!

Everyone in Boskyana calls Sundar 'Chachu', an honorific which invests him with an exalted status in the family.

He is made of hard rock. He is the captain of the ship. His

practice of many years was to go to Thiruvananthapuram for the summer vacation in May. After spending a month there, he would return to Mumbai sometime in early June.

I suggested a change in the timetable. I asked Sundar to get his wife and children to Mumbai instead. They would stay at Boskyana for a month; then Sundar would take them back to Thiruvananthapuram and spend some days there. And return to Mumbai.

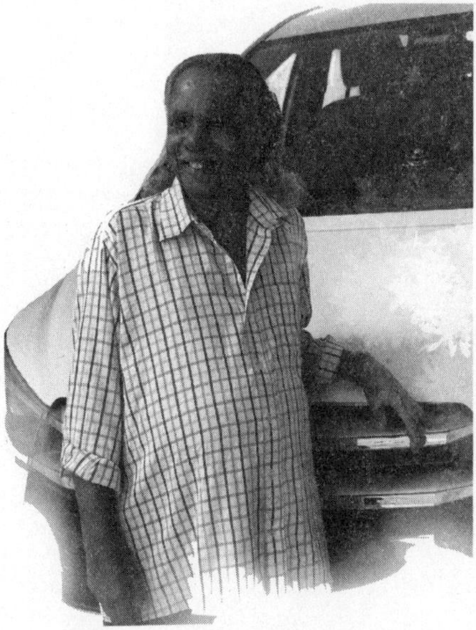
Sundar

Sundar has since stopped going to Kerala. He lost his wife and, later, a young son—in a gap of few years. His daughter is married and doing well in life. Sundar puts a video call to her once in a while.

Sundar has been with me for nearly five decades—fifty years is a long time. As he handles the household expenses, he is my finance minister—with no tax proposals, of course. He has of late grown his hair and the style suits him well.

My ardent wish is that Sundar shouldn't go anywhere as long as I am around.

Family Tree

Trees are the Almighty's messengers; every leaf is a hymn; every flower, a prayer.

It is said the earth was separated from the sun millions of years ago. The cooling process went on for, maybe, another million years. Subsequently, life sprouted from soft mud and soil: trees and leaves and grass and shrubs were the planet's first inhabitants.

If a blade of grass was the beginning of life, humans brought the magnificent process of evolution.

A fig (peepal) tree dates back to our ancestors. Its cells being akin to human cells—and also because it is rich with medicinal properties—the fig tree is worshipped. Carl Sagan has echoed such views in *Cosmos*!

In villages, life buzzes around a peepal tree. A sprawling one was the pride of our basti in Delhi—the Roshan Ara Baug. It provided cool shade to weary souls; elders would plonk themselves down on the stone enclosure and discuss everything under the sun; some would quietly watch the world pass by.

We would climb trees and collect mangoes, guavas and plum (jamun). Many trees were of my age; some, older, some young.

There was a black plum tree too. My mother and other women from the neighbourhood would sit under it and chat for a while. The Delhi summer can be ferocious. Children were told not to break the branches of the jamun tree, which looked like a wise, affectionate grandfather who keeps a kind watch on his brood. We would feel peace under his luscious shadow.

The jamun had a vast expanse; on one side stood the Fasih building, our house; on the other, a row of small houses. With its arms spread out, the jamun tree blessed us all.

However, the tree met a sad end during the Partition riots. There were large-scale killings and bloodshed. People mercilessly chopped off the jamun branches to burn the dead bodies—as if a father's arms were severed to perform the final rites of his children.

I wrote 'That Jamun Tree'—a story of how people trapped in hatred and malice lose sanity; the black plum tree symbolised the undivided India.

My love for trees is as fresh as a leaf. I have written many poems feting them; I feel elated in the company of Amaltas, Gulmohar, Masunda, Neem. When the breeze hums through a cluster of bamboos, it softly whistles '*saany saany*', as if in prayer. Poet Shailendra wrote a beautiful song for *Parakh*, a 1960 film:

'Mila hai kisi ka jhumka
Thande thande hare hare neem tale'

(Someone's earrings have been found
under the Neem tree)

I think the yellow Amaltas flowers resemble earrings.

I am growing old and have lost much of my hair. I wonder if the Roshan Ara Baug trees have lost their leaves?

My bungalow has a small garden. It commemorates the memory of Roshan Ara Baug. A Gulmohar rubs shoulders with the main gate.

Once it swooped very low during monsoon; it had to be firmed up. It was soon back on its feet, looking radiant with a red crown on its head.

I penned a song for a film:

Gulmohar gar tumhara naam hota
Mausam-e-gul ko hansaana bhi hamara kaam hota

Aayengi baharein toh, ab ke unhein kahana zara
Itna sune…
mere gul bina, unka kahaan bahaar naam hota
Gulmohar gar tumhara naam hota...

My garden boasts a tree which my wife, Rakhee-ji, gifted me years ago. We looked after it, watered it, but it wouldn't grow. We wondered why. Rakhee-ji had an answer. She said, 'Water, sunlight, manure is OK; but one should talk to trees. This is a tradition in Bengal. You have to converse with them. Trees are like babies.'

I started talking to the tree and how it grew! Now it looks sturdy and huge. Whenever Rakhee-ji visits me, she makes it a point to spend some moments with the tree.

I have a Masunda and white Champa too. When fully grown, the Champa branch or leaf oozes a white milk-like substance. So for me, Champa is the 'badi maa' of our tree family.

The Champa has a special trait: its leaves disappear when flowers begin to bloom and vice versa. The hide-and-seek game is exhilarating. Both leaves and flowers play on the shoulders of badi maa. There was a papaya tree too; it bears fruits only thrice and perishes.

Have you seen forest trees shedding leaves? They give up their verdant green and flaunt a range of colours—lustrous red, shocking yellow and crimson. In hilly regions, the Mahawa and Chinar trees resemble a wedding 'baraat'!

The moon too turns a pale yellow—ready to fall on my lawn like a withered leaf!

I must tell you about this poem which I wrote a couple

of years ago. A Safeda Cheel (an eagle with a head of white feathers) tree, perched on a hill, recounting the story of the once prosperous forest:

There once was a mango tree; the Koyal would come every spring, sit on its branch and break into a lilting melody. Sadly, the Koyal no longer comes as the mango tree has vanished.

Here was a cluster of bamboos. A crisp breeze would whistle through it. A little further was the deodar (Cedar)—proud and tall—so tall that one thought he wore a turban of clouds, says the Safeda Cheel.

Once in a while, the cedar would wrap itself comfortably in a shawl made of his own leaves. It would hold the hand of the breeze and swing gently in a rhythmic cycle. The deodar telling the breeze that were his legs not rooted in the soil, he would have joined him in his wanderlust?

The old Safeda Eagle talks of the three gulmohars which once thrived in the forest. Two of them have disappeared. One survives—defaced by reckless tourists who scribble their names on its trunk.

Right next to the gulmohar was the neem tree. The leaves would gradually turn blue when intoxicated by moonlight. The thick foliage, which added to the beauty of the faraway hill, is gone; humans destroyed it, set it aflame. The champa too is no more. Four or five eucalyptus trees are surviving. Just about.

I am reminded of the Chipko Andolan, which marks a watershed in our crusade to protect forests. Thousands would hug a tree in the Himalayan region to stop contractors from felling it to make way for big dams. Trees are the life and soul of a society and humans.

When travelling, I make it a point to leave home in the

small hours of the morning. The sun is all set to roll out and birds sing an ode to the forest. My eyes are fixed on trees lined up on both sides of the road.

Soon, I get lost in the journey of another kind.

Bosky

I wanted a girl child, while my wife Rakhee-ji and her close relatives were yearning for a boy. My driver Pandey-ji was my strongest ally.

I had always wanted to be a father to a daughter. Only a girl asks her father to tie her ribbon in a flower-like knot. A boy would announce jauntily that he was going out to play—and that's that. Boys are boys.

'Don't demolish my concept of a boy, please,' Rakhee-ji pleaded as our debate dragged on for days—baby girl or baby boy. Finally, I and Pandey-ji won.

I lost my mother when I was a year old—maybe, even less. I don't have with me a single picture of her. This may have sparked in me a wish for a girl child.

The newborn baby looked gorgeous and delicate—like a piece of soft silk. I called her Bosky. Rakhee-ji found it a bit odd. However, 'Bosky' was happily accepted by the family. There was a fresh debate when we were planning a formal naming ceremony.

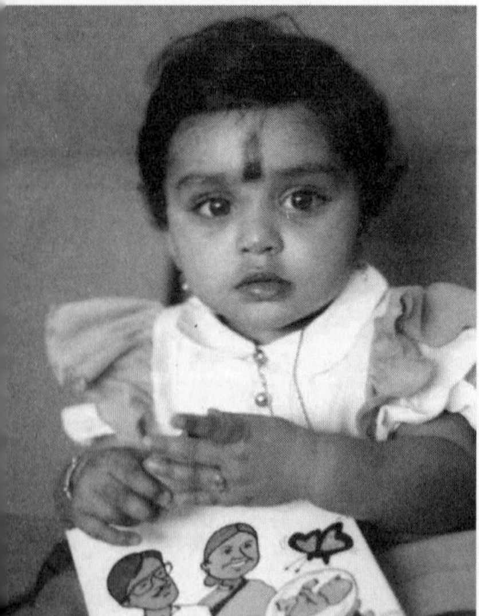

My eldest brother came up with Nishaat—a good name, I thought.

I suggested Sujan, my mother's name. Perhaps, the near-unanimous verdict was that you can't give your daughter her grandmother's name.

Close relatives were keen to uphold the family tradition. Sujan was thus rejected. Rakhee-ji suggested Meghna, a river which flows through her native town in Bengal.

I liked the name as much for its cadence as also for the fact that Rakhee-ji wanted to revive her link with her birthplace. Rakhee-ji belongs to East Bengal, now Bangladesh, while Punjab is my birthplace, now Pakistan. We often joke that Bosky is the only Indian in the family!

Seeing a child grow up is a wonderful experience which no screenplay writer can dare to put on paper. A baby keeps playing with her mother's pallu. Is it because she likes the weave of the pallu or its crimson colour? Who knows?

It was great to see Bosky take her first baby steps, mumble her first word. Dr Cama and Dr Gokhale, who heralded Bosky's arrival into this world, taught me how to wrap a newborn baby. I realised it was an art as exquisite as a Mughal miniature painting, and required great skill and patience.

I learnt to change nappies. It's heartwarming to hold a baby, close to your bosom. It oozes the sweet fragrance of life. While sharing the young one's universe, where elephants fly and trees pirouette, parents re-live their own childhood.

Bosky was ready to start her school life. I took her to several schools in the neighbourhood, but she liked none. I had some free time as I was freelancing during those years.

One morning I took her to a school in Khar, a quiet Mumbai suburb. She instantly liked it, and began to play with children. Her teacher Pinky, a sprightly, young girl, walked up to me, greeted me, and said, 'Sir, my father knows you.' Pinky was the daughter of Pran Sahab, the legendary actor.

The Khar school was held under the roof of an idyllic bungalow. Classes were conducted on the turf. Bosky joined the school, and stepped into a new world. Later, I and Rakhee-ji got her into a proper school.

Times were a tad difficult as Rakhee-ji was busy with her films. She often had to go out of Mumbai for outdoor shoots. Jethi, a good soul, was appointed as Bosky's nanny. She took good care of her for over a decade.

Bosky never needed a special tutor; she would study on her own. Neither I nor Rakhee-ji wanted her to be a topper. We gave her the space she needed; she was into sports, and acted in school plays too. I tip my hat to Ms Khariwala, the headmistress, who believed that a student's natural instincts need to be honed.

I've never imposed my choices, ideas and biases on Bosky. She worked on her own goals; carved her own path. I was, of course, there to provide inputs, whenever necessary. It was she who chose her subjects for graduation.

Weaving Bosky's hair into two plaits was a daunting task. I asked her if she could give me some tips. She would say, 'Papa, you don't know how to do it. You keep running the comb here and there.' I would remember my childhood days, when my father used to do my hair, like a Sardar-ji.

I've written many poems on Bosky. Every year I would present a poetry book to her on her birthday. She was too young to read and understand literature, but she found the cover and sketches fascinating. I must say that I could write children's books because of Bosky and her birthdays. I learnt a child's language at different ages, how it changes.

It's a tad difficult to write a book for kids. You have to keep reminding yourself that you are writing for young readers. I would tweak a folktale or a *Panchatantra* story. I wrote birthday books for Bosky for thirteen long years.

Actually, I came to know myself better while trying to understand Bosky. I learnt a lot from her. There was constant give and take between us. It is pointless to cast your child in your mould. A doctor's daughter need not brandish a stethoscope; she can wear a lawyer's white band if she so wishes.

I can recall how Rakhee-ji was keen that Bosky's college should be close to our home. I promptly dismissed the suggestion. Let her choose her own college, even if it is away from home, adding, 'You aren't going to sit with her in the classroom.'

We would drop her to school by car, but such occasions were few and far between. Like millions of Mumbaikars, Bosky would travel by local train with her friend to St Xavier's College in south Mumbai.

Parents need not hover over their children like a noisy helicopter. Their generation can meet the world with confidence—and on its own terms. They choose their friends, and if trust deepens, they consult them on matters of mutual interest.

Bosky was keen to learn swimming. I taught her how to get under the skin of the water.

While I was around to allay Bosky's doubts, I never meddled

with her studies or daily regimen. Once in a while, she would look grumpy and sullen.

Teenaged children have their own priorities, pressures and pangs. As they are on a crossroad, they need to be handled with care. Parents too face an acid test during those crucial years. You can't pacify a sixteen-year-old rebel with a toy train. A poem may help, perhaps:

Bosky is miffed with me, I suppose
A part of the body is quietly quiet,
Feet look swollen
And the way she looks, thinks—like the eye of a whirlpool,
She is staring
Bosky, a piece of sun,
Mingles in my blood, day and night;
Does she know that when she is angry
The blood in my vein stops running
Will she ever know?

I have countless memories of Bosky's childhood. Her mother knew many Bengali poems. She would take Bosky to the balcony and tell her, 'Come chandamama (the moon) to put a bindi on Bosky's forehead.'

Bosky would be amused.

Once, she went alone to the balcony, and saw half a moon. She said, 'Maa, *chandamama toot gaya*… (is broken).'

Although Bosky spent many years abroad, she never thought of settling there. She is firmly rooted in her soil. She loves India, its people and culture. She loves to play Holi, and actively participates in Durga Pujo.

Having majored in sociology, she has an abiding interest in social psychography—communities, customs and cultural practices and so forth.

Never saw Time come and go
Never saw the Revelation descending
Yet, I saw Time frozen in a corner
It perhaps entered with feet of dreams—softly, unobtrusively,
And when Time came, the intellect was not alert
The day I saw the changing colour of the eye
I kissed, but didn't recognise Time;
Heard soft echoes in her baby language
Saw Time when she lost her first milk tooth
Bosky, my daughter, soft as silk thread,
Wrapped in silk, lying lazily in silk
Never realised that Time is right there
When I placed her from the cradle on the bed
Washed her with lullaby words
Trimmed her growing nails
Bangles would slip in and out of her wrist,
And books, from her hands
Never knew that Time was engraved in words there
Never saw Time come and vanish
But saw him grow
This year Bosky will be eighteen

At eighteen, Meghna joined college. New horizons were expected to unveil before her—and unveil they did.

Govind breezed into Boskyana like a gentle wind, and before long became part of our clan. Both Meghna and Govind met at St Xavier's College as students. Soon, love blossomed. However, both handled the earlier phase of togetherness with admirable restraint.

Both went abroad for further studies and returned to Mumbai with their priorities well set for themselves. Both were totally focussed on their career: Bosky in cinema, while Govind, armed with a business management degree, was chosen for a key slot in TCS.

Back then, marriage was not a matter of hurry for them. But for their parents it was a source of worry. Meghna and Govind tied the nuptial knot in 2000.

A Punjabi from Patiala with a large head and a larger heart, Govind is imbued with confidence and camaraderie. He is our 'go-to' man, the ultimate multi-tasker who combines technology with practical wisdom to get things done.

A keen chef, his Mirchi-Mutton is tempting—a delectable treat for the family and his Doon School friends. His wide range of pickles makes Geeta-ji, his mother, lick her fingers. She is an incorrigible achaar addict.

Quiet, gentle and a tough man, Govind has been a great source of strength for Meghna. He juggles between home and office when Meghna is busy with her shooting schedules. Both have allowed each other enough space to evolve, to decipher the calligraphy of life.

The years Rakhee-ji, I and Bosky spent together is our shared legacy. We both have been a part of Bosky's life.

My book *Raavi Paar* has been published recently; I have dedicated it to Rakhee-ji:

'For Rakhee—the longest short story of my life.'

Pukhraj, my collection of poems, is for Bosky. The dedication slip reads:

Bosky bitiya,
A few letters from dreams are in this,
A few mirrors of the moon,
And sun's rays;
In the envelope of my poems are my experiences
And my blessings, my prayers;
Keep this with you when you set out to travel
They may be of some use, somewhere—perhaps

My Life, My Samay

A grandchild is Time's gorgeous gift to wrinkled hands and greying hair. A tenuous bond that links the past and the future.

Every father looks forward to his daughter getting married and graduating to motherhood; in the case of son, fatherhood.

We all see our grandparents, meet them, love them as naana-naani or dada-dadi. They become a part of our life. Remember, the grandmother in *Pather Panchali*? Her eyes, aglow with unadulterated affection, follow Apu and his sister wherever they go.

I spent my childhood in Dina, which is now in Pakistan. Kala, my naana's village, was just a stone's throw away. I would often meet my naana-naani in the market of Dina. They never called on us. I would visit them in Kala.

My naana would give me an anna (ik-anni); once my naani gave me two annas (du-anni)! My family members pulled my leg with a limerick.

Punni ka aa gaya naana,
Punni ko de gaya anna;

Punni ko mil gayee naani
Punni ko de gayee du-anni

I was called Punni at home.

An anna won't do with Samay, my grandson. Tech-savvy that he is, he wants to download a game. I ask him to take it up with his father.

'He isn't giving me any money. You give.'

'How much?' I ask.

'I don't know,' he answers in English.

I plead Samay's case in his father's court.

'How many games does he want to download every month?'

Govind asks me not to indulge Samay. 'Don't give him money,' he says. I promptly reject my son-in-law's suggestion. Some video games cost a thousand or two. So what?

Samay, my grandson, is Govind's heartbeat. However, the father in Govind never allows his affection for Samay to spiral out of control. Govind knows that a young, restless boy needs to be helped with inputs to nourish his world view. Both father and son get along like two boys on a playground, kicking goals and kicking up a storm.

In fact, Govind often chides me for indulging Samay with video games. Needless to add, I am unrepentant.

Samay charges Rs 50 from his parents for cleaning his room. However, he promptly doubles his remuneration when asked to spruce up his father's room.

'Why this hike?' I once asked him.

'Because Papa make more kachhra, Naanu,' he replied.

Samay returns Rs 100 to his father and asks him to download games for him.

'This isn't enough,' his father points out.

'Well, use your card. It doesn't require cash.'

As children, we used to buy 'revadis' and groundnuts in a pice; now children clamour for video games. However, affection can't be valued in terms of money. You have to be a grandpa or grandma to realise this. Ask me.

Times have changed; technology has brought the world

closer. Language and race barriers are fast disappearing. Today, a child is exposed to myriad influences, thanks to the latest communication devices. The grandparents-grandchild bond has stood the test of time. Ask Samay.

I often thought that a newborn baby was like a new planet joining a family's solar system. However, I soon realised that Samay was the sun, while we all were planets orbiting around him.

Samay:

Thought it was a small planet; born into my solar system
My grandchild—Samay;
Hardly two years old—yet I feel

That he is the sun—and we all
Spin around him;
What great gravitational force love has!

When Samay was a baby, I would try to spend more time with him. I would love to rock his cradle. Whether asleep or awake, he would be under my care. His grandmother too would be with me. We both would take turns to look after him, change nappies, clean his bed.

I would take him out in the evening—he, a bundle of joy ensconced in a cosy, little pram. I would show him birds and trees. Soon, Samay began to like pets. He has a great love for dogs. He began to train them. He enjoyed it. We were happy.

My poem 'Meghna' talks of my state of mind when my daughter gave birth to Samay. Like every father in the world, I was restless as I couldn't share Meghna's pain. Only a woman can bring into this world a new life. During those critical hours, the father is utterly helpless.

I was watching the Sea
My little pot of nectar was to emerge from the sea;
The sea turned sides, water was choppy,
Delicate pangs passed through the womb of my daughter
I was afraid to ask for nectar
I would shudder when she shivered

Although thirsty, she was not supposed to drink water
Small ice cubes were moved on her parched lips;
The sea was struggling within
Split the sea and bring out the nectar pot
If not, the girl would die

Now when she plays with the nectar pot
A man within me tells me:
'Man, you lacked the courage
To suffer pain and help create a human soul.'

When a daughter goes through labour pains, the father realises that he would remain a father forever; that he can't be a mother.

Yet the father in me has a mother in him.

Samay's childhood years brought immense joy to us. On joining school, he had a strong urge to be a teacher. We were his students. I put up a chalkboard for him in my room. It's still there. After his first visit to a doctor's clinic, he wanted to be one. We all were ordered to be his patients.

He would scribble nonsense rhymes on the chalkboard and paint the wall. Once his mother chided him. I reminded her that she was no less. She had once painted the ceiling fan with her Holi colour sprayer, I told her. She laughed heartily.

I was Bosky's mother when she was a kid. Now, Samay's.

Children are creative and perceptive; their tiny minds work like a beehive—in top gear: ready to understand, grasp, absorb and interpret. A child learns his/her mother tongue without a grammar book. We can teach children only if we are willing to learn from them. How they talk, play with idioms and ideas.

Once, I heard Samay saying, '*Zor lagaa key...*' He said '*Jor*' instead of '*Zor*'. I told him the difference. He didn't take too long to understand the subtlety of pronunciation.

Meghna laughed and said, 'Papi, I'll teach him all this; but what about his father? Who will teach him?'

I am a great advocate of the mother tongue. English is fine during office hours, but when at home you should speak to your children in the mother tongue. Meghna strictly follows the rule.

A child develops an affinity with words. Samay took an instant liking to a phrase he had heard from his father—'*Kya fayeda*?' (What's the use? What's the gain?). Such phrases are used just like that.

Samay clasped the word. 'Kya fayeda' became his catchphrase.

'Samay, go for a bath.'
'Kya fayeda?'

'Samay, change your clothes.'
'Kya fayeda?'

'Samay "Potty" pe baitho.'
'Kya fayeda?' and so forth.

Rakhee-ji hails from Bangladesh, while I am a pre-Partition child born in Pakistan. Meghna and Samay were born here in Mumbai. They are Maharashtrians—so am I, now that I live in this city. Samay has learnt Marathi in school. It's nice to hear him converse in Marathi with Meghna's staff—'*Kaay pahijey*?' (What do you want?).

Samay is a symbol of pluralistic India.

Rakhee-ji speaks with me in Bengali when she wants to discuss confidential matters. Samay is amused. 'You are talking in Bengali, no?' he remarks. He doesn't understand Bengali, though. I am sure he will soon learn the beautiful language.

The new generation is more well informed than their grandfathers. They know about stars and constellations, birds and beasts, rockets and mummies, dinosaurs.

Rakhee-ji has told Samay about different species of fish, how they travel from salt water to freshwater lakes, how they lay their eggs. Grandma is his close friend. They fight once in a while. Grandma meets him on his ground—like his school peers. I lack the tact.

I don't consider myself Akbar, the great emperor. But Samay is my Shekhu—my Jahangir, and I will never deprive him of the love of Anarkali.

1.

This 'Cozihom' slope is too steep for me
To walk up or descend; I am an old man now,
Time knows—Samay yeh jaanta hai
I held his hand as he got down from the school bus,
Samay wanted to alight on his own

He was restless to meet his favourite cat along the narrow road.
I held his schoolbag and water bottle;

Samay said, 'Give me the schoolbag, Naanu—and hold my hand; you may trip and fall.'

2.

Samay...
It has been long since I played with you with a poem

Why the hurry to be an adult?
Do some silly pranks sometimes
We like your childhood
Let food fall on your clothes,
Fight with Naani,

Hear scolding from mother, but...
You've started saying Sorry, OK and Thank You—
And to crown it all you were talking on 'aab-o-hawa' today;
Samay—you looked so innocent
We like your childhood!

Pali

Pets are pure happiness. They make us better humans; tolerant and compassionate. To tell you the truth I was never a great friend of dogs. Rakhee-ji once brought home a cute, little dog.

Bosky, my daughter, taught us to love pets. Young kids and pets make great friends.

Once Bosky came home with two little puppies and a school friend in tow, and declared with the earnestness of a child, 'Papa, I want to have a pet. What should I do?' Her friend belonged to a family which sold pets.

I had a close look at the puppies. Their sinless, virtuous eyes moved me deeply. I was in a fix. What if I keep one of the two? The second one would go to some other family. I dislike separation. I told Bosky, 'We'll keep both.' She was on cloud nine. The two puppies too seemed happy. They knew it was their home.

Bosky came up with names: Chhotu and Motu. For a decade or so she shared her childhood with both. The troika would fill the house with joy. Chhotu-Motu became our kith and kin. *Mere apne.*

Gradually, Chhotu began to age. He looked frail and tired. His life was ebbing away slowly. It made us sad. We gave him the affection which a senior member of the family deserves.

Meanwhile, Motu disappeared. A bolt out of the blue. I had just returned home from an outdoor shooting. Motu was nowhere to be seen. Actually, he would be the first to greet me; his tail wagging at a frenetic speed, his eyes dripping affection.

Motu must be around, playing and having some fun in the courtyard, I thought. Motu anyway had a habit of sneaking out for an hour or so; but he would soon be back home like a good boy.

However, this time around he didn't.

Next came Pali. His story is both nerve-wracking and heartwarming.

Eager to sell two Boxer pets, a gentleman put an ad in newspapers. Bosky brought both the pets home. She gave one to Raakhee-ji, the other was to be with me. We started calling him Pali. He was cute and playful. Everything was smooth and fine for a month or so.

All hell broke loose one day when we realised that a dog-lifter had made good his escape with Pali. Bosky was distraught. Worried, she began to run from pillar to post, zeroing in on places where dogs would be illegally bought and sold.

I was aghast when she told me about such centres tucked away in Mumbai's shady by-lanes. She was ready to move heaven and earth to get back Pali.

Often, someone would call up to share some information. Even on a sketchy clue, she would rush out of home. She got in touch with members of the canine society; put up posters with Pali's photograph emblazoned it, all over Pali Hill, and wrote a moving article in *Bombay Times*. It went viral.

A good samaritan rang up at 3 in the morning one day to say that he had read her *Bombay Times* piece, and that he had just returned to Mumbai from New York. 'I would certainly help you locate Pali,' he said. His words soothed Bosky's wracked nerves.

The man who stole Pali belonged to a well-knit gang. However, he met his nemesis in his father who had read Bosky's *Bombay Times* article. He took his son to task, saying that he would no longer keep stolen dogs in his house.

The father rang me up, 'Sir, your Pali is with us. My son will bring him to you within an hour. Kindly forgive us.' We all were happy. The world is a nice place to live in, I thought.

Pali came home. I could see suspicion lurking in his eyes. He wasn't willing to trust humans any more. For days he wouldn't go out of the gate. For days Bosky stayed home to pacify him. She would play with him, feed him, shower love on him.

We consider Pali as one of us. I have told my domestic help to treat him as one would treat a family member.

My day is made when Pali comes rushing to the gate to greet me after I come back from my morning walk or a game of tennis. He starts playing with my shoe lace, pulls down my white stole and starts munching it.

Pali is too classy to eat cheap biscuits; he would eat the same ones which I ate with tea. Ginger biscuits from Keyani's, Pune. He loves to feast on jamuns; like me he too relishes sweets, and ice cream. He plays with Thakkar Singh and Joy, my close aides. He sits next to me when I am at my writing desk, eagerly waiting for a warm pat from me every day.

I'll tell you a hilarious story about Pali. A writer once came home for a story session. True to his type, Pali inched closer to him and started sniffing—every dog's way of getting to know a stranger.

No sooner had the writer begun to read the story, Pali began to snore heavily. The writer was nervous. I told him, 'Don't worry; keep on reading. Pali loves to give his opinion.' He really did—regardless of the literary merit of the story!

A few years ago, Pali fell ill. His eyes turned pale and he began to shrink. He died in my arms. A small statue of him adorns my office where he used to sit.

He lived his full life of fourteen years. I had just finished the last page of my book for Penguin's *Another 100 Lyrics*. I dedicated the book to Pali, with his photograph.

PALI

Hiding, in some dark... corner
She was watching
Pali was a bit weak and sick

She snapped at him, and took him away.
She eats everything...
Death has no caste
Creed or moral!

Keekar

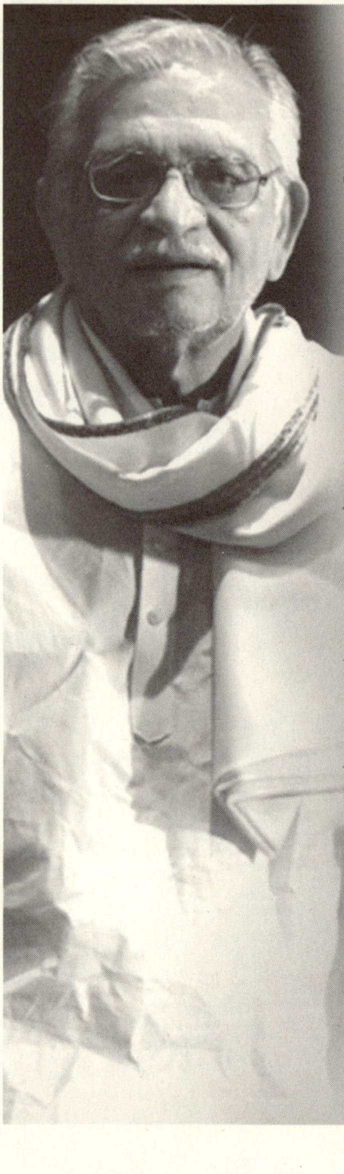

There was a Keekar forest

There was a Keekar forest
Once, lightning struck, and
Know not how, only one Keekar was seized
Others survived;
Still, the lone Keekar stands amidst
others—badly charred

Now, a lot of people come to see it,
They touch it and feel it
And are flummoxed

Often, in the night's deep silence
All other Keekar exchange whispers:
'What was so special about it
That it alone was struck by the bolt?'

Zero Line

I wrote a song for *Parichay* (1974):

Musafir hoon yaaro
Na ghar hain na thikana
Mujhe chalte jaana hain
Bass chalte jaana

Forever on road,
forever walking.
That's life.
Footloose and fancy-free.

Travel is of two kinds: within and without—both crucial to life. One helps us decode the world unfolding around us every hour; the other equips us to grapple inner demons.

My life's journey began in Dina (now in Pakistan) on 18 August 1934. Eighty summers on, I remember Dina: the mud roads; the nice little railway station; Abbu (my father), my friends and tender trees which lent grace to the idyllic village. Childhood years enrich you, deepen life's meaning.

My house in Dina (left) and Dina Railway Station (below).

Partition tore me away from Dina. The family came to Delhi. I joined a school in Delhi. However, Abbu thought Mumbai (then Bombay) would do me good. He sent me off to my brother.

I was supposed to stay with him and pursue studies. You can't imagine how edgy I was when the Maximum City opened its doors for me. Bombay: A heady brew of hope and despair, real and surreal.

Life began to unwrap me. My ties with the family were strained. I wasn't informed about Abbu's death. My brother took a flight to Delhi to attend the last rites.

A week later, Samuel Tunius, our neighbour in Delhi, wrote to me, saying that Abbu was no more. I was working for Bimal Roy Productions. Bimal-da asked Pirachand, his manager, to arrange for my Delhi ticket. I was miserable during the Bombay-Delhi journey.

I told myself—I will be on my own. On returning from Delhi, I left my brother's home. New life, new journey. Bombay turned me into a lone pilgrim.

> 'एक अकेला इस शहर में, रात में और दोपहर में
> आब-ओ-दाना ढूँडता है आशयिना ढूँडता है'

The journey continues...

Over the years I have travelled across the length and breadth of the country—no big plans. Everything was decided in a jiffy. Before you could say 'statue', I would be out on the road, driving on highways.

On most days, writer Bhushan Banmali would join me. The nights would be spent in dak bungalows—a charming legacy of the British Raj. At the crack of dawn, we would hit the road.

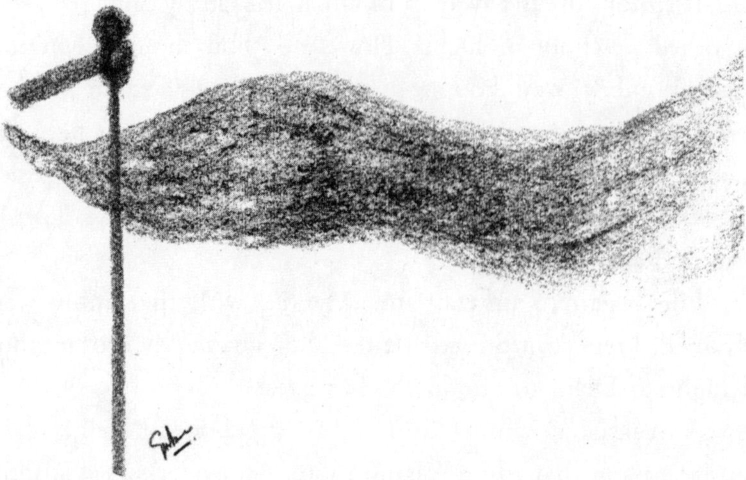

Film festivals have taken me to cities far and wide. There have been some unplanned sojourns too. Way back in 1967, a devastating earthquake wrought havoc in Koyna, a village near Pune. It is pointless to sit home and read news reports of the tragedy, I told myself. Next, I was on my way to Koyna.

My wanderlust reflects in my poetry as well. In *Pandhrah Paanch Pachattar* you will find poems capturing the mood of the cities I have been visiting. To me each metropolis gives a different image.

For example,

Madras (Chennai):

This city looks old, weather-beaten;
It has started expanding
Like the bloated belly of an old man.

Mumbai:

Lying on water like a large, long fish,
This city
Its head in water, feet resting on the land;
Neither would it leave the sea, nor get into it
This city of Mumbai.

New York:

Why would your city—oh friend,
Not have a single house of ants?
Never saw any ant at all,
Even when I dropped a little sugar on the floor;
None came,
In our village homes we spread some wheat flour
If we see a row of ants marching by a wall.

The Delhi Afternoon:

When Delhi would be roasted in debilitating heat
He would appear on the scene
The charpoy-weaver
And raise a cry from the corner of the 'ghanta-ghar' (clock tower);
One hand placed firmly on the ear,
'Make charpoys...make charpoys...'
Those sleeping behind the 'khuskhus' curtains, the Delhiwallas—
Would know—it's one-thirty p.m.

Kolkata:

Have you ever seen...
Underneath the staircase of a building
Where an electricity meter-box is fixed,
Old and rusted—
Under its open cover are kept some fuse plates
Which look like paan-stained teeth
But the light never goes off, in this live city.

The poet keeps close tabs on the city and its people—with empathy and certain aloofness. I can't explain the entire process, but a poem often takes shape while I am travelling. Both are intertwined, I suppose.

We were on our way to Nashik. As is my wont, we left Mumbai early morning with my friend Arun Shevate. We both had breakfast under a tree on a wayside dhaba. It was nice to see so many celastrus of trees crammed with tiny, beautiful flowers.

We resumed our journey. Sundar was at the wheel this time. A little later, we lost our way, or so we thought. I began to feel the pangs. On a copy of the *Times of India* I wrote:

Come, let's roam about these treacherous lanes
And take a look at
Squares of sly streets
I've heard that people who Time squeezed and abandoned
Have settled here
They are the skins of life
Drops of their extract is in your body—like poison.
As Time will kill more such people...
Come on, let's roam about these treacherous lanes

Here's yet another example of how poetry fuses with travel. I was on my way to Mulund, a Mumbai suburb, for a literary event. My friends Ashok Bindal and Arun Shevate joined me. I could hardly see traces of old, sepia-tinged Mumbai. The city has changed beyond recognition, I told myself. We three got talking, but memories of Mumbai refused to go away.

These Were Villages Then

These were villages once—
Mulund, Bhandup, Bhiwandi
Innocent, smeared with slush;
Mulund, Bhandup and Bhiwandi
Like little girls they frolicked in the woods;
And sea would carry salt to the bay
Each resembled a village.

A drain overflowing,
A fragile brook hanging by a rock
As you passed through a field or a pathway
Everyone looked similar
These were our villages once

Now—all have become Mumbai's clones
Mulund, Bhandup and Bhiwandi—all
They are big-ticket cities
They stand on their toes stylishly

Some have built glass apartments;
Some, artificial gardens

Somewhere you find municipal schools made of stone
Some have put boxes upon boxes—high malls!
You can step in for tomatoes, green peas—and motorcycles too.

Mulund, Bhandup, Bhiwandi have mutated into glittering cities
They don't meet up;
These are the new faces of Mumbai
Less characters, more actors!

I was a young boy of ten or twelve when I left Dina, my birthplace. I visited Dina recently—in my sunset years; after seven long decades. My school, my old house, roads and pathways, the bazaar—and Abbu, my father came to greet me. Grey images began to float before my eyes. I returned to Mumbai and wrote:

Walking in measured steps towards Wagah
I stood on the Zero Line, while
The sun was behind me
My shadow was back in Pakistan!
My father stood before me
He saw me...

His walking stick rested on the ground
He smiled, and said,
'When I left the dust there
I had returned home, Punni!'
(My father would call me Punni)
'I knew you would come, Punni,
You didn't know of my death
I was so sure you would come to bid me goodbye.'

A dazed pause.
Abbu tapped the stick again gently on the ground
Extended his hand and said,
'Chalo, let's go to Dina.'

Friends who had come to Wagah to receive me
Held my hand, and led me to Lahore instead.

Amidst the city's din and clamour
No soft voice to greet me
But I could see a road of eternal silence
It went to Dina.

A tiny township
Once a railway station
Made of cardboards;

All trains wouldn't take a halt there
But those were the World-war days
Trains with a special salon for soldiers would stop;
Seeing a line of smoke, I would rush to the station
Abbu would step out, carrying lots of things for his shop

There was a market

A road—
It's still there
And a 'madarsa', where I would sit on a jute carpet and write on a wooden plank;

My mind is probing Dina;
A small by-lane which opens to a field
I touch walls, on which I had scribbled, in coal, something in crystal-pure Urdu

I thought someone would hold me by hand
And teach me spellings;
None came
I perhaps left him at Wagah

I am back,
Here I am—on the Zero Line
My shadow is behind me, it calls out:
'When you leave your dust

Come over, your home is here
Your motherland...your watan.'

As I look back on the years gone by, I realise that my wanderlust kept me going—from nothingness to nothingness, from one zero to another.

A Night to Remember

Night is both a fact and fantasy. Night is an idea and image. Night has appeared in many of my poems and songs.

The night tiptoes quietly
Silent, the night neither cries nor laughs,
Like a blue dome it seems to be flying in the air
Or like an empty houseboat, it keeps floating;
Moon beams don't seem to be wearing their everyday silk
Moon—as if a slippery twig, slithers like soap,
And a sandstorm of quietude is stirred
If you could, for once, wake up from sleep
And see what goes on during the night of separation

In many of my poems I have tried to demystify night and moon. '*Mora gora ang layeeley*', my first song, was a tribute to the magic of night. I have a collection of poems—'*Raat, Chaand Aur Main*' which talks of the night's myriad moods.

Down the years I have travelled a lot—four thousand kilometres or more. My usual practice is to set out at the crack of dawn—watch the sun unveil a ravishing dawn, and hear melodies of our winged friends.

By evening we reach a destination and unwind. Travelling through the night in ethereal silence can be a remarkable experience—both beautiful and bizarre. And pleasant too. Sample this one:

I drove from Delhi to Hrishikesh, where a friend of mine told me that a big dam was soon to come up at Dev Prayag. I thought of visiting the town before it disappeared into deep waters.

My friend gave me a nice travel bag stuffed with blankets.

'It's quite cold out there,' he said. Bhushan Banmali and Taran, both dear friends, were with me.

I must say that the journey from Dev Prayag to Anand Prayag was fascinating: zigzag roads, beautiful valleys and hair-pin bends amidst dazzling, snow-capped mountains.

Somewhere along the way, we met a soldier, Bhola Singh Sandhu, who too was going to Anand Prayag. As he asked for a lift, we offered him a seat. He was jovial company like any soldier and a Punjabi on top of it. His family lived there. He insisted that we should spend the night at his house. However, we politely declined his invitation, dropped him at his destination and zoomed off.

The dak bungalow sparkled with old-world charm reminiscent of the British Raj. The security guard welcomed us with a warning that there were no spare rooms. His response to every question we asked was an emphatic no. I put my long experience as a roadie to good use. 'Was Major Bakshi here?' I asked the security guard, 'He has booked the room,' I added, sounding firm and no-nonsense.

The trick worked. The guard opened a large room for us. In a short while Bhola Singh's envoy came with a huge tiffin carrier stuffed with piping hot food. Yummy!

The next day we left for Joshi Math. Bhushan Banmali suggested that we should instead go to Badrinath. 'We can stay at Joshi Math,' he added. The rising sun looked, to quote an Assamese folk song, like a mighty tiger on the prowl.

There was snow everywhere—as far as the eyes could see. Snow and tall trees. Dew-fresh serenity was strewn everywhere. On our way to Birla Ashram (where we were supposed to stay), we bought a mud stove and coal. Quilts and mattresses were available on hire, in the Upper Bazaar, where we parked the car and went down the valley, to Birla Ashram.

The cold was terrible. When we came up again, we found a small note glued to the wind screen: 'Further down is a petrol depot; to the left is the military mess. Please join us for a meal —Bhola Singh Sandhu.' Three cheers for Bhola Singh Sandhu!

The dinner was fabulous. Everyone had rum, and we heard evocative Urdu couplets and rib-tickling jokes from sturdy soldiers of the fabled Punjab Regiment.

As Bhushan had a drop too much, they fed him gulab jamuns. I tell you it was a hilarious evening.

We returned to Birla Ashram and began to walk down the road. I heard someone say in a sing-song manner:

Step
Step
Slope
Step

That was Taran. An inebriated Bhushan was feeling terribly cold, and he was unsteady on his feet too. It was pitch dark and Taran was reminding him of the descending steps.

Step
Step
Slope
Step

We finally reached the ashram and made Bhushan lie on bed, wrapping him neatly in a blanket. The weather was damp and the coal wouldn't catch fire. We used newspapers as fuel. But not for too long.

Taran had a brainwave: he thought of pouring some brandy on coal so that it caught fire. A flame, bathed in blue, began to flicker, looking like a simmering sapphire. I and Taran heaved a sigh of relief.

Taran remembered his classroom physics. 'The room is closed and so are the windows. In the absence of ventilation, we will soon be gasping for breath,' he warned.

The door was opened—just a little, a few inches or so. Adversity makes a person industrious. We tied a suitcase to the door with pyjama drawstrings to prevent it from banging shut. Lucky Bhushan! He was fast asleep.

The cold continued unabated. Some more quilts were heaped on Bhushan. As midnight drew to an end, I and Taran gulped down the remainder of the bottle and crashed out.

Our first task in the morning was to check if Bhushan was OK. 'I am perfectly fine—but, you know, all through the night someone kept piling heaps of luggage on me,' he said.

The night made my day!

The night in the mountains is something else
The sky is never switched off
And the river is resplendent with light
One can see the dazzling 'zari' work done by stars
Like a city looks from the aircraft.

Nearby is the river, a black band fastened on eyes
Runs around, playing and singing:
'Koda Jamaal Shahi, aaye jumme-raat aayee,
peeche dekhe shaamat aayee...'

The breeze, with a comb held between its teeth, makes lot of noise

Broken and frail
Like an adolescent boy

Two waterfalls converse with each other in a loud voice
It's like meeting two village pals
Who keep asking about people back home
Poems sleep with eyes half-open
The night in the mountains is one of its kind

Writing Cinematically

I began writing poetry and fiction much before I took to film-making.

I make a film because I want to say something. The human relationship triggers my imagination. The human mind is a web of relationships—some clear as a sun-lit day, others hazy like a pale evening.

Relationships are awash with colours which share a rapport with music. I am happy when I am able to weave musical notes into my poems or films, and happier still if viewers share my joy.

Every human experience is suffused with 'rasa', which nourishes a work of art. Rasa takes one to the ultimate truth. I image for truth.

Film-making is often likened to a ship set afloat. It's the director who decides the destination. It is true that artists, cinematographers and technicians are part of the journey. Actually the director too is a crew member, but he is the captain of the ship.

The director's expertise is just a device to navigate the vessel through choppy waters. Of course, the director has to navigate the vessel to the right shore for which the ship started the journey.

The director is responsible for communicating to his viewers, with clarity, the thought which he had conceived. Sometimes even the best of thoughts lack communication.

Viewers are the film's final arbiters. Never ever did I doubt the collective wisdom of the people. Viewers are not well versed with the technical intricacies of a film. Their verdict depends largely on whether the film resonates with their personal experiences. If they like a film they praise it unhesitatingly. Viewers are unbiased. Watching a film is a collective ritual.

Hence, there is no room for bias.

An experience can't be untrue; similarly, views too can't be untrue as they stem from experiences. You have to speak with a young boy in a language he understands.

Film-makers often attribute their failure to popular taste. Actually, this is just an alibi.

Making thoughtful, human films has been my ambition. Through films I wish to express my idea of life, my worldview, my experiences. Take, for instance, Satyajit Ray. His films are marked by intensity and poignancy—the two factors that define great cinema. They are loaded with experiences of life.

Many stories keep humming at the back of the mind. Some are yet to ripen—maybe, they are waiting for the opportune moment. I don't like to force myself on my ideas. Once the gestation period is over, thoughts break open the shell and appear on the scene. Creativity is like a fragile flower. You can't trample upon it. It will bloom at its own pace, unmindful of the world and people.

For instance, a Japanese film called *Happiness of Us Alone* touched me deeply. It stirred my thought.

I didn't have any inclination of joining films then. It's a long story now. I landed in films many years later. I learnt the craft under my guru Bimal Roy. When I became a director. Later, the thought of the Japanese film still lingered on. I thought of writing down a script by the name *Koshish.*

Koshish is the tale of a differently abled couple; both husband and wife can neither speak nor hear. I wasn't worried if I would succeed in transmitting the dialogues between the couple to the laity. I think silence gives birth to art—writing dialogues is an exception. However, it is equally true that being able to transcend beyond written dialogues is an artistic accomplishment of the highest kind.

While doing the drafts of my film scripts I concentrate on my characters, not viewers. There are other things in *Koshish* which speak with eloquence.

For instance, music, lights, camera. How does a differently abled boy convey his delicate feelings to a differently abled girl; how does the husband-wife duo create a space for itself in the so-called 'normal' world; how do they lead a life which is more serene and beautiful than the one led by a normal person. This is the theme of *Koshish*. I am of the firm view that differently abled persons deserve our respect. Mere compassion is sentimentalism.

Actually, the *Koshish* couple transcends beyond its disabilities; they clock in more hours of work and toil harder than others around them, thus becoming good citizens. This is *koshish*.

I think form is immaterial after a point. Whether you are writing a short story or doing a film, your central protagonists are not of much relevance—they may be ordinary citizens or belong to royalty. Much depends on whether you have portrayed them with honesty, whether you've touched the life's aching nerve.

I use humour and poetry in good measure in my films as I am fond of the two rasas. I think humour and poetry fill one's life with happiness. Often, a common man is steeped in high-class poetry. I use the two rasas in good measure—but not as a box-office formula.

Portraying a character with intensity is a tough task. As I look back, I think I didn't tackle the intricacies of Anand's character, in *Anand*, with the empathy it deserved. Next came *Bawarchi*. You will find that Rajesh Khanna as and in *Bawarchi* connects with *Anand*. The two share a bond. Did I write Bawarchi's character to undo the wrong which I did to *Anand*? Viewers don't pay attention to such details. However, the writer keeps sulking.

Friends and admirers often ask me—what if I hadn't joined the world of cinema. Well, I would have looked for alternatives to express myself. I think I've a lot many things in me apart from literature, which I need to express.

If films did not exist, I would have searched for another medium as powerful, all-pervading and far-reaching as cinema.

As a film-maker I was never a taskmaster; that's not me. There are many insecurities in life. However, work soothes my nerves. I feel re-charged after a gruelling day on the floor. Work makes me feel secure and safe. I love my work and I think it shows in my work.

Bimal Roy is my icon. No one can surpass him in the devotion of film-making. Today, a good film inspires me first; then the film-maker. I mean the director.

Oops! I Stepped on a Dream

Ambarish had a couple of things to tell me. 'Humans are puzzled by dreams. They can't yet figure out the whys and hows of this strange trick which sleep plays on them. Do dreams transmit a meaning? Are they real?'

'Well, I think dreams are real. They are born, at some level, in the deep folds of our consciousness, and are part of our existential baggage.'

Ambarish pressed his point further. 'Huzoor, aren't dreams as real as inflation and power cuts? They are solid. Pure gold. The contents may be spurious. So what?'

I read out to him one of my poems:

Montu Roz Hi Bore Hota Tha:

Montu would get bored every day
When Papa would tell him the Naani story
While patting him to sleep, every night
'And that old woman...on the moon...
Is a Jagat Naani
Seated on a charkha
She spins clouds…

You know her, Montu—don't you?'
By which time Montu would turn over
And fall asleep;
Once Montu couldn't sleep and Papa
Began the same old Naani story

'Do you know, Montu...
That old woman who lives on the moon
And turns the spinning wheel...?
My grandma used to say that

she was her great great-grand mother...'

Montu yawned and said,
'Had you told Armstrong about her
he would've met your Naani!'

Ambarish smiled and said, 'A dream and fantasy are thick as thieves—if you send an SMS to dream, it is quite likely that fantasy may reply. Imagination is the third partner in the alliance,' he said, adding, 'Poems have a dream-like quality. It takes in its majestic sweep dream, fantasy and imagination and sets out to meet the ultimate truth.'

Here's another poem:

Tiptoe quietly along the way,
Mind your step—
I have, in the depth of my loneliness,
laid out several dreams
If one of them wakes up
It will die

Not all dreams are beautiful. Some are awful, fearful—even hideous. Partition shattered my childhood. For many years, I would see blood and devastation in my dream, and many familiar faces, which kept mutating. Eventually, all faces, hazy and blurred, would merge. I would wake up, horrified.

There was this dream—unremittingly scary: I am lying near the gate of my school. My hands and feet have been chopped off. A man with a turban quietly walks up to me. He has wrapped himself in a blanket. He caresses me softly and says something in whispers. I can't understand a word. The man crosses the nullah near the school and disappears.

Why have they torn off my limbs? And that man—whoever he may be, but his presence there at that point of time was reassuring. The man looked like one of my school teachers and also like the grandfather of my school friend Jaggi. My father too used to wear a turban.

All faces gradually fuse into a blurred circle.

One more dream. A boy who used to lead the school prayer is being taken away by a man who carries a naked, blood-stained sword in his hand. People are running helter skelter amidst violence. However, I am unable to run away to safety. A petrifying nightmare.

Often I dream that I have been gheraoed or chased by an angry mob. Terribly scared, I am gasping for breath. Doors, roads, staircase, balconies—everything seemed like a mammoth trap.

Dreams emerge from a constant churning of life, experiences and memories. Dreams do a lot of good work too: they cleanse our system, purge us of our angst and anxieties; offer us some breathing space and unburden us of our woes and worries.

Who can stop a poet from seeing dreams in broad daylight? I often see myself stepping on clouds and dreams. Clouds are smashed to smithereens, dreams suffer deep cracks—and I trip and fall.

I was busy with the script of *Mausam*. I just couldn't figure out how to take the film to its denouement. One evening I consulted my colleagues. We had a long chat. Thereafter I finished my meal and went off to sleep—tired and exhausted.

However, my mind was buzzing like a beehive. I must have been in half-sleep, swaying between mindfulness and deep slumber, when the *Mausam* climax began to bleep on the mind's screen. In detail.

Friends often ask if a poem has ever appeared in my dream. It is the other way around. A poem first enters my consciousness and then meets me in a dream.

Ambarish broke his silence, 'Suppose you meet your beloved in a dream. You would wonder if she too has seen the same dream. Not possible, but cinema can make it possible with the help of songs. A film lyricist can "hear" his dreams through songs lip-synched by actors.'

'I suppose my song in *Golmaal* will prove my point.'

Ik baat kahoon, gar maano tum
Sapnon mein na aana, jaano tum
Main neend mein uthkar chalti hoon
Jab dekhti hoon, sach maano tum;

Kal bhi huwa tha ki tum gujare the paas se
Thode-se anmane, thode udaas-se,
Bhaagi thi manaane neend se lekin
Sofe se gir padi,
Ik baat kahoon gar maano tum

'I am sure Sigmund Freud would have gone crazy reading these lines,' remarked Ambarish.

A song from *Kinara* offers some valuable tips on dreams:

Ek hi khwaab kayee baar dekha hai maine
Tuune saari mein udas lee hai meri chaabeeyaan ghar ki
Aur chali aayee ho bas, yoonhi mera haath pakad kar
Ek hi khwaab kayee baar dekha hai maine

Mej par phool sajate huwe dekha hai kayee baar
Aur bistar se kayee baar jagaya bhi hai tujhko
Chalte-phirte tere kadamon ki woh aahat bhi suni hai
Ek hi khwaab kayee baar dekha hai maine

Gungunati huee nikali hai nahake jab bhi
Apne bheege baalon se tapakta paani
Mere chehere pe chhitak deti hai tu Tiku ki bachhi
Ek hi khwaab kayee baar dekha hai maine

Taash ke patton pe ladati hai kabhi khel mein mujh se
Aur kabhi ladati bhi hai aise ki bas khel rahi hai
Aur aagosh mein nanhein ko liye…
'Will you shut up?'

Aur janati ho Tiku—
jab tumhara yeh khwaab dekha tha
Apne bistar pe main
us waqt pada jaag raha tha

I see dreams even when I am wide awake. No need to close my eyes. What if you don't dream? Don't worry. One can see, feel and touch dreams any hour of the day. Dreams add colour and fragrance to life, regardless of whether they materialise or not. We see dreams and will continue to do so.

Let this dream of mine come true.

The Making of a Song

Hindi films can't do without a song. Moreover, cinema connoisseurs love to hear stories of how songs are made; their trajectory from a modest harmonium to the recording studio and thence to the silver screen. Frankly, I am not quite good at this.

Nevertheless, let me give it a shot.

At the outset, I must say that I was never enamoured of films. I was into reading and, later, writing. I migrated to Mumbai from Delhi to pursue my studies, but ended up joining Vichare Garage, at Belasis Road, in the Bombay Central area. The job suited me fine as it gave me ample time to read and discover Mumbai.

There were some film personalities, including Basu and Debu, who I knew from IPTA and Bombay Youth Choir. Debu was looking for some place to live, and thus landed up at my one-room lodge at Coover lodge, Andheri.

It so happened that Sachin-da (SD Burman) had a tiff with Shailendra-ji and opted for another lyricist for *Bandini*. One thing led to another and Debu took me to Bimal-da. Coincidences happen not just on the silver screen.

Bimal-da and Sachin-da explained to me the mood of the song. Leading lady Kalyani (Nutan) is in love with Vikas (Ashok Kumar), but she can't bring herself to express it. The song happens on a night when Kalyani, seated by a mud stove, comes out of the kitchen and in a flush of love and freedom begins to hum.

A big argument ensued between Bimal-da and Sachin-da. Bimal-da didn't want Kalyani to step out of the house, while Sachin-da insisted that she has to go out of the courtyard. The debate went on for a while.

'If Kalyani isn't coming out of the courtyard, the song will get choked,' declared Sachin-da.

Next, Bimal-da briefed me about the 'situation': It's pitch dark. Kalyani is afraid to step out. In keeping with the prevailing custom, she shouldn't be seen in the village at an unearthly hour.

Next day Sachin-da played the tune for me.

Lalala la lalala lala la...
Dadada da dada da lala la

A faint sketch of the song began to flicker before my eyes, regardless of the beat and tumble of the studio. Few '*lalala la*' and some '*dadada daa*'. A tad nervous, I geared myself to recite my lines to Sachin-da. He began to hum, even as his frail, long fingers moved gracefully on the harmonium notes. Some truncated words were linked together.

Dui chaar pug...Bairi kangana chhanak naa...

I used the jumbled lines as pug; more words followed, some images too.

Bairi kangana chhanak naa

Sachin-da sang the tune aloud for me. It entered my consciousness, drop by drop. I stored it in my mind and began to think of Kalyani: What must be weighing on her mind? How would she cope with her predicament? Unexpressed, silent love. A deep urge to break into a song at night.

Kalyani is looking at the moon. The moon is smiling. She curses the moon:

Tohe rahu laage bairi
Muskaaye jee jalayikey

Kahaan ley chala hai manwa
Mohe baawari banayikey

Kalyani is lost in thoughts: What if there was no moonlight? If I wasn't fair-skinned. I would have merged into the night.

'Mora gora ang layeeley
Mohe shyam rang dayee dey'

My first song had night as its backdrop or 'situation'. Six decades of my journey continues—in search of night, the moon and the aching urge for eternal love.

Lockdown of COVID-19: Poems

COVID-19: Migrant

Dry leaves fell off from the branches of the trees
Winds kicked and scattered them all over the garden,
This time around the autumn visited the motherland—
With a strange bearing

Many crushed on pathways in cities
Many lost in dust and cloud, and storms,
Many buried under the nameless coffin debris,
This time around the autumn visited the motherland...

Those which came hurtling down—couldn't reach the roots
They had great hopes—Alas! Couldn't touch the earth
They burned, and burned this time in the fire of life
This time around the autumn visited the motherland...

Batwara
Partition – Migrating

They were rushing to their villages, back to their motherland
I saw similar caravans back in nineteen forty-seven

We, too, had fled from our villages towards our homeland...

It allowed us in, labelled us refugees, and the state offered us shelter

Now, they are stopped at state borders,
For giving refuge is dangerous

Back then, there was the hour of death which wanted to know your religion

Today, too, the killing hour of death stalks them,
Irrespective of religion, name, caste
—It kills

Which Partition is more gruesome?
This, or that?

It Was a Pandemic

All labourers, artisans, fled home
The city's machines had begun to screech to a halt
These had kept them going,
Actually they had sown their lives in their village fields

A piece of land—one, two, or five acres,
For everything was there, sowing and mowing

Jowar, rice, maize, bajra—everything
The split of land—with kith and kin
Quarrels, by canals and drains
Cudgel-men, sometimes ours, sometimes theirs

Those legal battles between family elders—naana, naani, and daddu
Engagement ceremonies, weddings, granaries,
Drought, flood, erratic monsoons.

Will die where there is life.

Just that the bodies were plugged here

Everyone pulled the plug,
'Come, let's go home'—and go, they went...
Will die where there is life.

COVID-19: A Day

When the sun rises
I rush to the boundary
And catch a day, daily.

I smell the day for a while,
Like a blood orange freshly plucked

For a while I examine before peeling it
To check if the day's dimensions are intact—not less;
If there are as many hours as every day

I swirl it on my hand like a globe
All maps fly around like rumours,
Skins of stories
Time peels off, layer by layer

Bland leisures subside
Memories seek and hide,
Like the drawers of a desk;
From winnowing paper baskets
I toss and chuck countless words into my mouth.

And then...

In my hands the day starts melting
Palms start reddening,
When the day warms up
I begin to huff and puff

I cut with knife and fork
An hour, an afternoon, and moments.

By evening the day
Starts drying,
The remainder I pour in a drink
And keep sipping

When sleep kicks in,
In sleep the day will be declared out;
Yet another day of lockdown.

Dhoop Aane Do
Let Light In

Immensely sweet, beautiful—this earth,
We know, it's a lump of jaggery

Dangerous winds have descended;
Let not worms feast on this earth,
Move away, wait a while,
Let light in

The sun will rise, and filter with its rays,
The baneful winds

Like insects, don't huddle together,
Stand away from each other

And let light in

Women in Films

'I have to look for words when someone asks me how well do I know women. What do you mean by "knowing"? Just a nodding acquaintance?' Gulzar asked.

I had come to him with a cartload of questions.

Excerpts:

'Let's talk about the woman you've portrayed in your films.'

'Which woman?' he asked, his eyeballs glued to the television screen which was showing a riveting cricket match.

'A woman you saw...'

'What do you mean?'

'Are you OK?' I asked.

'Absolutely. Age plays its tricks, though,' he laughed.

'Elaborate, please.'

'Well, I am yet to join the Old Men's Club where toothless crackpots rave and rant about women for hours over beer. You can put this question to me after I cross sixty.'

'You may have turned senile by then, *"Sathiya gaya"*—as they say in Hindi. Do you think people will stop nagging you because you are sixty?'

'No,' Gulzar interrupted. 'My point is all that we see and know need not be expressed in words.'

'Cowardice, isn't it?'

'Maybe, I don't know. But how would you prove the truth? Actually what we say in words isn't the truth—what we conceal, is. Every woman is someone's mother, sister and wife. Imagine a stranger boasting that he really, really "knows" a woman. You know what I mean? In that macho way. There are some who like to brag. Who's going to like it? I? Your husband?'

'Don't talk in riddles. A woman's fragrance lingers on for long in your writings and in your films. Would you agree?'

'If I say yes, you will try to pin me down to define the relationship; if no, you will call me a liar. So, silence is best.'

'This isn't fair. This ostrich-like attitude of yours. One needs a source of strength in life.'

'But, it's so iffy-iffy. Nothing is certain.'

'True, but hope never dies,' I pointed out.

I think I had struck a chord. Gulzar began to talk on issues germane to creativity, and its highs and lows. To me it seemed like a moving soliloquy by one of India's finest poets. Read on:

There's just this delicate line of fragrance—and nothing else. It's better not to contaminate it by touch or a relationship tag. Let the fragrance 'be', let the feelings 'be'.

I am essentially a storyteller. As I write, I keep changing a few lines, tweak a word here and a line there to keep the pace of the plot going; to keep intact the rhythm and beauty of experiences and emotions as well. Actually I had never thought that my passion would be my profession. Believe me.

Life is linked with material needs. When I left home, I was keen to know everything about life. However, little did I know then that my creative urge would collapse under the burden of material needs—the time-tested truth called salt and bread.

The day I gave up the security of hearth and home, the high castles of ideas and ideology came crashing down. Hunger stared me in the face. It followed me everywhere. Very Dickensian, you know.

I think a writer is in no way different from a daily wage earner—say, a carpenter, plumber or a vendor. However, by the time I realised this it was too late. Those who gave a big push to my ramshackle bandwagon when I set out on my life's solo journey were the ones who held the reins. They showed me a land of dreams cultivated not by them, but someone else, and said in a syrupy voice: 'Look dear, your task is to make this carpet look gorgeous; but don't tamper with the design, OK?' The world sets its own rules.

The colours I once stole from life have now dried up. I think I've lost the ability to re-invent myself, renew myself. How on earth will my characters be true to life? Hemingway would often say that when he sits by his typewriter, he tells himself that if my first line is born out of truth—pure, unadulterated, stark, then I can go on writing till the cows come home. A writer's quest for truth makes great literature.

Gulzar took a brief pause. I could see Lord Buddha, cast in marble, meditating on a mantlepiece.

I turned nostalgic. The *Bandini* shoot had just resumed at Mohan Studios after a long hiatus. *'Mora gora ang layeeley'* had turned out to be a sensational hit, and Bimal Roy's fourth assistant had become a famous lyricist.

However, the lanky poet with mesmerising eyes loved solitude. Unlike the film fraternity, he kept away from the glitz and glamour of tinsel-town: the jostling crowd, autograph-hunters, meetings and seminars, and the paparazzi.

Away from the hurly burly of the shoot, he would retire to a quiet corner and write beautiful poetry. He would often seek shelter in my mother's (Chandrima Bhaduri) office and get lost in his own world of imagination. Needless to add, the *Bandini* poet I am talking about is Gulzar.

We resumed our conversation.

'Is it true that in your early years, you wrote for the sheer pleasure of writing, and later to keep the home fires burning?'

'That's OK. You write because you want to keep your body and soul together. However, if you take a macro view then literature is all about feelings and imagination. Valmiki hadn't met Lord Rama; Ramayana happened because of Valmiki's exceptional creative power and fertile imagination.

Look, there are no clever calculations in literature. Also, literature goes beyond grammar—pronouns, prosody and blah blah blah. Imagination breathes life into characters and situations.

'Can one say that you portray a woman on celluloid without as much as knowing her?'

'I'll give you an example. Take, for instance, a mirror. We fall over each other to see ourselves in the mirror. Does the mirror go searching for its own image? It's the consciousness that matters. I portray consciousness as woman—and vice versa.'

'Wouldn't you ever admit that you have understood women?'

'Tell me, how can a woman conceal herself from the world around her? Everyone knows her. Every musical note (sur) is suffused with her grace and beauty. She is everywhere—homes, fields, offices, universities, streets and by-lanes, gardens and railway stations.'

'As a poet and film-maker you can de-mystify a woman at a much deeper level.'

'For instance?' he asked.

'Say at the level of love and pain?'

'The thing is if you try to discover a woman beyond her name, social status, educational qualifications and so forth you come to a point when you get nothing except bones and flesh—not even a drop of blood. Ossified rituals and regressive traditions keep hovering over her head like hungry vultures. There is nothing left except a skeleton.'

'There you are. You have eventually de-mystified a woman, haven't you?'

Even as I say this, I am reminded of one of Gulzar's poems:

Treading cautiously amidst thick trees sometimes
And sometimes hidden behind the city's walls
The night has saved herself from cowriwallas;
Clutching tightly a moon-coin of eight annas in her hand,
She quietly steps out of home;
To visit the morning fair
Oh! this innocent, poor little night.

Gulzar seemed in a dilemma—his mind eager to relax, but heavy with thoughts and images.

'One thinks of escorting the night to the morning fair and buy her a few toys,' Gulzar said, a smile lighting up his deep-set eyes.

'What name would you give to a woman who has come into her own after a quick conversation with adolescence—would you call her radiant?'

'No, I would call her a symbol of self-respect. Take, for instance, the character of Kusum in *Khushboo*. In *Parichay* I tackled the concept of self-respect, which peaked in the character of Aarti in *Aandhi*,' Gulzar explained as evening turned into a soft, velvety crimson.

'Tell me about the woman from your film *Khushboo*. Why should she feel compelled to marry the hero?' I asked.

'Because of a small crack in self-respect. The anger at not having gained what one had aspired for often ends in helplessness or submissiveness. Life is all about combating our quirks, foibles, our qualities as humans or, as a last resort, coming to terms with them,' he said.

'Why should you run away from human relationships when the expanse of your consciousness is so vast?'

'Time doesn't wait for anyone. Nor does it genuflect before anyone. Time doesn't need endorsement; it is a great, vast force, a never-ceasing torrent. Similarly, you can't detain or define your sense of touch, taste and smell. Then why the need to invest it with a name?'

'Like sorrow consciousness too doesn't carry an I-card. It doesn't have a pin code. Touch, smell, sorrow, love, joy belong to all—and yet to none. These things can't be earned, acquired, flaunted. Similarly, it's pointless to harness them or place them under the yoke of tradition,' he pointed out.

I realised that Gulzar was at his best.

'We all say that a shadow never leaves us. But it does when the sun sets in the evening, or a lamp's flame is extinguished. This is life's truth. Why should we be surprised about all this? Your eyes may be open, but you may not have the nazar to perceive the world.'

Elaborating on the topic, he said, 'In the absence of consciousness, you can merely set your eyes on a continent of darkness. But consciousness will enable you not only to "see" but "hear" darkness—and "smell" its fragrance too. This is identity. Mine and yours.'

'Enough for today,' he signed off.

Amen, I said to myself.

Interview conducted by
Ruma (Bhaduri) Sengupta

Sufi

Some, wearing beads around their neck, still wander around the world singing their prayers.

This is spiritual, Roohaani. We call them Sufis or Sufi songs and rhythm, without a destination of religion or culture.

A soul never arrives in this world, or leaves it, flaunting a mark of faith.

A 'baul', Lalan Shah Faqir, is addressing God as he sings:

Mere ghar ki chaabi kisi aur ke paas hai
Main dekhoon toh kaise?
Mere ghar mein daulat chhupi hai
Joh raazi ho durban
Toh darwaaza khole
Magar usko pehchaan sakta nahin main
Bhatakta hoon andhere mein
Main andha janam ka, main dekhoon toh kaise?
Mere ghar mein daulat bhari hai

Har insaan mein ek heere-saa mann hai
Joh pehchaan ley woh
Usee ka woh dhan hai,
Lalan kahe:
Main andha janam kaa, main dekhoon toh kaise?
Mere ghar mein daulat padi hai

Lalan loves to engage with human beings—their happiness and sorrow, their struggles, foibles and failures, travails and triumphs. Human life is the keystone of his poetry and his philosophy. He abhors rhetoric, he condemns rituals. He keeps away from the gobbledygook of 'atma' and 'parmatma'. He is concerned about this world, life sprouting everywhere, every minute. He wants to make this planet an abode of peace and harmony.

Lalan's poetry drips with sweat and tears. He believes in a simple life, few needs. He says:

Ek anjana panchhi kaise
Pinjre mein aata jaata hai

Haath agar aa jaata toh main,
'Mann bedi' pahana deta
Panchhi key pairon mein;
Ek anjana panchhi kaise
Pinjre mein aakar ud jaata hai

Aath kothri, nau darwaaze
Beech mein jaaliyon ke parde hain
Aangan paar, sadar ghar andar
Sheeshe aur aayeene jade hain

Kismat ka pher nahin toh kya
Mujh se panchhi aisa salook karta
Seekhein tod pinjre ki
Door hi door udaane bharta?

Pinjre ke bharose tha tu manwa
Kachha baans tha pinjre kaa
Rota kyoon hai ab tu Lalan
Yaheen pe toot ke bikhrega

Ek anjana panchhi kaise
Pinjre mein aata jaata hai

Lalan utters elementary truths without much ado. His words are rough-hewn—his style, unadorned. His writings reflect his social concerns. He believes that the body is the way to know the Universe, and the Universe exists in the body. Lalan Faqir celebrated his philosophy in the eighteenth century—born in 1770, he lived for 116 years as said in some records.

Bulleh Shah, another Sufi singer, was born in 1680.

Like Lalan, Bulleh Shah too talks of mankind's everyday struggle.

Both speak in one voice. Shared values obscure socio-cultural differences: A thread of cultural unity and harmony runs through their works, regardless of region and culture. It's interesting to note there is a gap of a century in their lives, but the social concern remains the same.

Bulleh Shah Poems:

1.

Bulleya ki jaana main kaun
Bulleya to me, I am not known

Na main momin vich maseetaan
Na main vich kufar diyan reetaan
Na main paakaan vich paleetaan
Na main moosa na firown

Not a believer inside the mosque, am I
Nor a pagan disciple of false rites
Not the pure amongst the impure
Neither Moses, nor the Pharaoh

Bulleya ki jaana main kaun
Bulleya to me, I am not known

Na main andar ved kitaabaan
Na vich bhangaan na sharaabaan
Na vich rindaan masat kharaabaan
Na vich jaagan na vich saun

Not in the holy Vedas, am I
Nor in opium, neither in wine
Not in the drunkard's intoxicated craze
Neither awake, nor in a sleeping daze

Bulleya ki jaana main kaun
Bulleya to me, I am not known

Na vich shaadi na ghamnaaki
Na main vich paleeti paaki
Na main aabi na main khaki
Na main aatish na main paun

In happiness nor in sorrow, am I
Neither clean, nor a filthy mire
Not from water, nor from earth
Neither fire, nor from air, is my birth

Bulleya ki jaana main kaun
Bulleya to me, I am not known

Na main arabi na lahori
Na main hindi shehar nagauri
Na hindu na turak peshawri
Na main rehnda vich nadaun

Not an Arab, nor Lahori
Neither Hindi, nor Nagauri

Hindu, Turk, nor Peshawari
Nor do I live in Nadaun

Bulleya ki jaana main kaun
Bulleya to me, I am not known

Na main bheth mazhab da paaya
Na main aadam havva jaaya
Na main apna naam dharaaya
Na vich baitthan na vich bhaun

Secrets of religion, I have not known
From Adam and Eve, I am not born
I am not the name I assume
Not in stillness, nor on the move

Bulleya ki jaana main kaun
Bulleya to me, I am not known

Avval aakhir aap nu jaana
Na koi dooja hor pehchaana
Maethon hor na koi siyaana
Bullah! ooh khadda hai kaun

I am the first, I am the last
None other, have I ever known
I am the wisest of them all
Bulleh, do I stand alone?

Bulleya ki jaana main kaun
Bulleya to me, I am not known!

2.

Ranjha Ranjha kardi ni,
Me'n aapay Ranjha hoi,
Sado ni me'n no Dhido-Ranjha,
Mano Heer na akho koi,
Ranjha me'n vich me'n Ranjhay vich,
Mayko'n hor dhiyan na koi,
Wakho loko Heer Slati,
Kithay aan khaloi.

Repeating the name of Ranjha
I have become Ranjha myself.
O call me ye all 'Dhido-Ranjha',
let no one call me Heer.
Ranjha is in me, I am in Ranjha,
no other thought exists in my mind.
I am not, He alone is.
He alone is amusing himself.

3. Translation: by Kartar Singh Duggal

Aa mil yaar saarley, meri jaan dikhaan ney gyheri
Come my love take care of me, I am in great agony.

Mullan Qazi rah batawaan, deen dharam dey pherey
Aye taan thag jugat dey jhaar, lawaanjaal chufereey

The Mullah and Qazi show me the way,
Their maze of Dharma that is in sway.
They are the confirmed thieves of time,
they spread their net saintly crime.

Nadioon paar aye mulk sajan da, lehar lobh ney gheri
Satgor beri perhi khalotey, ten kion lai aweri

My Master lives on yonder bank,
While I am caught in the gale of greed.
With boat of anchor, He stands in wait,
I must hasten, I can't be late.

Bulleh Shah sho tenoon milsi. Dil noo dey dileyri
Pritam pass tey tolna kis noon? bhlioon shaker dopheri

Bulleh Shah must find his love,
He needn't have the last fright.
His love is around, yet he looks for Him,
Misled in the broad daylight.

Aa mil yaar saarley, meri jaan dikhaan ney gyheri
Come my love take care of me, I am in great agony.

The interconnectedness of the saint-poets is fascinating. For instance, the Maharashtrian saint-poet Namdeo has a wide following in Punjab. There is much in common between Meerabai of Rajasthan and the rebel women poets of south India. The cultural renaissance is deeply enriched our languages and dialects.

There is no marked line between the saint-poets who sang, and the Sufi singers, who wrote poetry.

But Sufi singers do appear like bauls. In my imagination and not vice versa. Yet a question comes to my mind. Rumi, a Sufi poet for sure. I can't call him a baul, but the rhythmic dervish dance in Turkish culture is quite close to it. Let me narrate a story to you. It's from the celebrated Urdu writer Joginder Paul.

A small refugee family lived in a refugee camp, after migration from Pakistan, in 1947. The old mother would go up to the gurdwara close by and hum her prayers every morning.

When things improved in some months, the family rented a small house and moved to another locality. But there was no gurdwara nearby.

A few months passed by and the elder son enquired one day.

'Maa, shall we find another house? You must be feeling lost. There is no gurdwara around this place!'

'No son. There is no problem at all. There is a masjid behind the house. I go every day. Bow my head. Hum my prayer and come back.'

I thought she was a real Sufi mother.

Acknowledgements

I would like to particularly thank Arun Shevate for painstakingly, over a period of several years, collecting these essays, articles and poems, and publishing them in the Marathi publication, *Ruturang*. It is because of his efforts that the beautiful Marathi version of *Dhoop Aane Do* came to life and eventually became the inspiration for the current English edition.

I will be forever grateful to my cool, patient editor Bidisha for answering my calls at all odd hours, with special mention to the time when she was in the hospital attending to her ailing father.

Gulzar